105

JFK and Sam

JFK and Sam

The
Connection
Between the
Giancana and
Kennedy
Assassinations

ANTOINETTE GIANCANA
JOHN R. HUGHES, DM OXON, MD, PHD
THOMAS H. JOBE, MD

CUMBERLAND HOUSE
NASHVILLE, TENNESSEE

JFK AND SAM
PUBLISHED BY CUMBERLAND HOUSE PUBLISHING, INC.
431 Harding Industrial Drive
Nashville, Tennessee 37211

Copyright © 2005 by Antoinette Giancana McDonnell, John R. Hughes,
and Thomas H. Jobe

Cover design by Gore Studio, Nashville, Tennessee

Library of Congress Cataloging-in-Publication Data
Giancana, Antoinette.
    JFK and Sam : the connection between the Giancana and Kennedy assassinations /
Antoinette Giancana, John R. Hughes, and Thomas H. Jobe.
        p.   cm.
    Includes index.
    ISBN 1-58182-487-4 (hardcover : alk. paper)
    ISBN 978-1-58182-487-2 (hardcover : alk. paper)
        1. Giancana, Sam, 1908–1975. 2. Criminals—United States—Biography. 3. Mafia—
United States—History—20th century. 4. Kennedy, John F. (John Fitzgerald), 1917–
1963—Assassination. I. Title: John Fitzgerald Kennedy and Sam. II. Hughes, John R.,
1928– III. Jobe, Thomas H. (Thomas Harmon), 1943– IV. Title.
    HV6248.G38G52 2005
    364.152'3'092—dc22   2005023354

Printed in the United States of America

1 2 3 4 5 6 7 8 9 10—10 09 08 07 06 05

To Lawrence H. Tayne, Melvin Pearl,
Robert J. McDonnell, and my five sons—AG

To Mary Ann Hughes, John Fino, Carrie Fino,
and my daughter and two sons—JRH

To Patricia Jobe—THJ

You can fool some of the people all the time,
and all of the people some of the time,
but you cannot fool all of the people all the time.

—*Abraham Lincoln*

Contents

Acknowledgments

Thank you, Lawrence H. Tayne, for giving me a break many years ago when I needed it the most. I have never forgotten you. If it were not for your help and guidance, I would not be where I am today. Thank you, Mel Pearl, for your guidance and caring. Thank you, Bob Mc-Donnell, for the important contributions you have made to this book. Thank you to all my family and friends for your enduring support. I am grateful to you all.—AG

I want to acknowledge the patience of my beautiful wife, Mary Ann, with her elegance and charm, and also my daughter, Cherie, for her interest and encouragement. John Fino contributed his technical in-genuity in dealing with tapes, disks, and photos, and his daughter, Carrie, retyped my manuscript over and over again. I want to also thank my excellent editor, Ed Curtis, and Marnie Ellingson for her ad-ditions.—JRH

Special thanks to the late Boris M. Astrachan, MD, for his support during a troubling time and for his passion for the truth.—THJ

Prologue

Wно can hear the words *grassy knoll* or *Texas School Book Depository* without a shudder of horror? Who can forget the handsome, smiling president waving to the crowds lining the route of his motorcade and the next minute his wife, in her brave pink suit, trying to hold his shattered head together? It happened too quickly. The nation was stunned, chilled. How could someone who seemed larger than life in one second be reduced to such a bloody death?

Neither can we forget the solemn funeral march in Washington, the riderless black horse, the dignitaries from around the world risking their own lives by walking unprotected past crowds of onlookers in order to honor our president.

No matter what sorry scandals have been revealed since, at that moment in history, John Fitzgerald Kennedy was our leader, much admired, energetic, elegant, a figure from Camelot, and he was mourned.

What threads of hatred tangled together at that spot, at that time, to lead him to a rendezvous with an assassin's bullet?

Most of the books dealing with this subject devote as much as 20 percent of their pages to hundreds of references to support each fact as it is presented. Although these references can lend a sense of credibility and coherence, we opted simply to provide a framework for Antoinette Giancana's recollections. We have decided not to supplement these with references, especially because so many of the numerous books on the Kennedy assassination already have this documentation, and our facts are similar to those already published as well as the huge documentary material released under the Freedom of Information Act. If readers wish to explore any point in depth, we recommended the following books that have provided so much of our data.

Brown, Madeline. *Texas in the Morning*. Baltimore: Conservatory Press, 1997.

Brashler, William. *The Don: The Life and Death of Sam Giancana*. New York: Harper & Row, 1977.

Church, F. Forrester. *Father and Son: A Personal Biography of Senator Frank Church of Idaho*. New York: Harper & Row, 1985.

Confessions of an Assassin: The Murder of JFK. MPI Home Video, UTL Productions, 1996.

Crimaldi, Charles. *John Crimaldi: Contract Killer*. Washington DC: Acropolis Books, 1976.

Davis, John H. *Mafia Kingfish: Carlos Marcello and the Assassination of John F. Kennedy*. New York: Signet Books, 1989.

Demaris, O. *Captive City*. New York: Lyle Stuart, 1969.

Exner, Judith Campbell. *My Story*. New York: Grove Press, 1977.

Giancana, Antoinette. *Mafia Princess*. New York: Morrow, 1984.

Giancana, Chuck, and Sam Giancana. *Double Cross*. New York: Warner Books, 1992.

Groden, Robert J. *The Killing of the President*. New York: Viking Studio Books, 1993.

———. *The Search for Lee Harvey Oswald*. New York: Penguin Books, 1995.

Hersh, J. M. *Dark Side of Camelot*. Boston: Little, Brown, Co., 1997.

Lane, Mark. *Rush to Judgment*. New York: Holt, Rinehart & Winston, 1966.

Livingstone, Harrison, and Robert Groden. *High Treason*. Baltimore: Conservatory Press, 1989.

Marrs, Jim. *Crossfire*. New York: Carroll & Graf, 1990.

North, Mark. *Act of Treason: The Role of J. Edgar Hoover in the Assassination of President Kennedy*. New York: Carroll & Graf, 1991.

Posner, Gerald. *Case Closed*. New York: Random House, 1993.

Prouty, L. Fletcher. *JFK: The CIA, Vietnam and the Plot to Assassinate John F. Kennedy*. New York: Carol, 1992.

Ragano, Frank, and Selwyn Raab. *Mob Lawyer*. New York: Scribner, 1994.

Roemer, William F. *Man Against the Mob.* New York: Fine, 1989.

Roberts, Craig. *Kill Zone.* Tulsa, OK: Consolidated Press International, 1997.

Russo, Gus. *Live by the Sword.* Baltimore: Bancroft Press, 1998.

Scott, Peter Dale. *Deep Politics and the Death of JFK.* Berkeley and Los Angeles: University of California Press, 1993.

Sinatra, Tina. *My Father's Daughter: A Memoir.* New York: Simon & Schuster, 2000.

Summers, Anthony. *Not in Your Lifetime.* New York: Shooting Star Press, 1998.

United States House of Representative Select Committee on Assassinations (HSCA). Investigation of the Assassination of President John F. Kennedy. Hearings and Appendices to Hearings, 12 vol. 95th Congress, 2nd Session. Washington DC: U.S. Government Printing Office, 1978–79.

United States Senate Select Committee to Study Governmental Operations with Respect to Intelligence Activities (The Church Committee). Alleged Assassination Plots Involving Foreign Leaders, November 20, 1975, 94th Congress, 1st Session. Washington DC: U.S. Government Printing Office, 1975.

United States Senate Select Committee to Study Governmental Operations with Respect to Intelligence Activities (The Church Committee). Final Report. Washington DC: U.S. Government Printing Office, 1976.

United States. Warren Commission. *Report of the President's Commission on the Assassination of President John F. Kennedy.* Washington DC: U.S. Government Printing Office, 1964.

JFK and Sam

1

November 22 as Reported by the Media

YOU REALLY NEED TO make a trip to Texas, Jack," more than one of President John F. Kennedy's advisers had recommended over the first six months of 1963.

The president didn't have to ask why such a visit was necessary. Most of his staff felt the trip was long overdue. He had made only a few brief visits to Texas since the 1960 campaign. In addition they hoped his visit might settle the dissension within the Texas Democratic Party well before the start of the 1964 campaign. This trip would also be used for some political fund raising.

On June 5, 1963, after addressing the cadets at the Air Force Academy in Colorado Springs, Colorado, the president flew to El Paso, Texas, to meet with Vice President Lyndon Baines Johnson and Texas Governor John Connally. Among the topics for their discussions was the plan for a presidential visit to Texas in November. Kenneth O'Donnell, special assistant to the president, was appointed coordinator of the trip.

As originally planned, President Kennedy would visit Dallas, Fort Worth, San Antonio, and Houston all in one day. News of his one-day visit was reported on September 13 by both Dallas newspapers—the *Times-Herald* and the *Dallas Morning News*. Although there was some criticism of the president's impending visit, both newspapers reported that Dallas officials were prepared to provide a warm welcome. The *Times-Herald* editorial on September 17 asked Dallas citizens to be "congenial hosts" even though Kennedy did not carry Dallas in 1960 and might not be endorsed in 1964. About three weeks later the *Dallas Morning News* reported that Congressman Joe Pool hoped the president would receive a warm welcome and would not be subjected to the hostility Lyndon Johnson faced during the 1960 presidential campaign.

In the days and weeks preceding the president's Texas trip, however, there were several ugly incidents in Dallas. Three of these raised considerable concern about the safety of the president while he was visiting Texas.

The first occurred on October 24. After delivering a speech in the Dallas Memorial Auditorium Theater, Adlai E. Stevenson, the U.S. ambassador to the United Nations, was jeered, jostled, and spat upon by hostile demonstrators. The demonstrations were publicly admonished by Dallas officials and both Dallas newspapers. But the Dallas chief of police anticipated more trouble. He ordered the assignment of one hundred extra off-duty policemen to provide additional security for the president. Dallas Mayor Earle Cabell pleaded with Dallas citizens to be on their best behavior throughout Kennedy's visit. He said Dallas was no longer the "Southwest hate capital of Dixie," a reminder of the city's reputation during the roaring twenties. Even the president of the Dallas Chamber of Commerce provided assurance that Dallas citizens would greet President Kennedy with warmth and pride.

Notwithstanding this shocking Stevenson demonstration, the president's advisers decided to extend the president's Texas visit to two days, beginning Thursday, November 21, and ending Friday evening, November 22. For Texas citizens this became official when, on September 26, both Dallas newspapers reported details of the president's revised two-day visit with Dallas as one of the scheduled stops.

The second incident occurred on November 21, the day the president was due to arrive in Texas. From out of nowhere, anonymous handbills designed to look like FBI wanted posters began to appear on the streets of Dallas. Each handbill contained two photographs of President Kennedy—one full-face, the other a profile. Under the caption WANTED FOR TREASON was an outrageously offensive bill of particulars whose only purpose was to smear the president.

The final incident occurred on the morning of the president's arrival. The *Dallas Morning News* carried a full-page advertisement with a black border bearing the caption, "Welcome Mr. Kennedy to Dallas." Following the caption were a series of dubious statements and questions highly critical of the president and his administration. The ad was sponsored by the American Factfinding Committee, an ad hoc committee whose only purpose was to place the newspaper ad.

When the president arrived in Dallas on November 22, Kennedy read this ad and handed the paper to his wife, Jacqueline, asking, "Can you imagine a newspaper doing this? We're headed into nut country now."

Other November events raised significant questions about the safety of the president. On the first of the month, an administrative assistant to Senator George Smathers of Florida, who was an usher at Kennedy's wedding and remained a close friend, wrote a memo to an associate outlining plans for a Kennedy visit to Tampa and Miami. Eight days later, Joseph Milteer, a political activist from the far right, had a conversation with an informant, William Somersett, and told him how he expected President Kennedy would be killed in the near future. He also said that the plan "is in the working." This information came from a transcript of the conversation received by an electronic device on November 9, 1963, by the intelligence unit of the Miami police department.

On November 21, 1963, Kennedy departed for Texas. Clint Murchison, wealthy oilman and original owner of the Dallas Cowboys football team, hosted a huge party to which he invited other well-to-do oilmen, including H. L. Hunt, one of the richest men in the world. Hunt allegedly financed the WANTED FOR TREASON handbills regarding Kennedy that began to appear on the streets of Dallas that day. Other dignitaries in attendance included Vice President Johnson, FBI Director J. Edgar Hoover, former Vice President Richard Nixon, and John J. McCloy, former U.S. high commissioner for Germany.

Why the party? Some have claimed that it was a celebration of the planned murder of Kennedy, in part because the president had earlier threatened to remove an oil-depletion allowance that would adversely affect the oilmen. In fact, Madeline Brown, mistress of Lyndon Johnson (who fathered Brown's one son, now deceased) later claimed that Johnson told her during the party the president would be assassinated. According to Brown, Johnson said, "After tomorrow, that's the last time those goddamned Kennedys will embarrass me again."

Such was the political atmosphere in Dallas on Thursday morning, November 21, 1963, when President John F. Kennedy and his entourage flew to San Antonio for the first leg of his whirlwind Texas visit. Upon his arrival in San Antonio, he was joined by Johnson and went straight to the U.S. Air Force School of Aerospace Medicine, the former Brooks Air Force Base, to dedicate a new research facility. Later he flew to Houston for a testimonial dinner honoring Congressman Albert Thomas. Then the president flew to Fort Worth, where he spent the night. In each of the three cities, the president's motorcade was greeted by friendly, enthusiastic crowds.

On Friday morning, after a breakfast speech before a large Fort Worth audience, President Kennedy and his wife, Jacqueline, flew to Dallas's Love Field, arriving there at 11:40 a.m. "Why are we visiting Dallas?" the first lady wanted to know.

Although the president truly enjoyed and looked forward to all public appearances, he reminded her, "I lost the city of Dallas in the 1960 election and I need to improve my popularity there." His advisers believed he could enhance his support by having his motorcade pass through downtown Dallas en route to the Trade Mart to speak at a luncheon planned by some business and civic leaders. Texas Governor Connally insisted that the lunch be held in the Trade Mart rather than the Women's Building, which was also considered. Jerry Bruno, President Kennedy's advance man, argued vigorously against having the lunch at the Trade Mart. He also insisted that the motorcade should proceed straight down Main Street without turns. Ultimately, the Trade Mart won out. After the luncheon the president was scheduled to fly to Austin to attend a reception and speak at a Democratic fund-raising dinner. The final stop on the president's busy itinerary was a visit to the ranch of Vice President Johnson.

With no threat of rain that Friday morning in Dallas, a "bubble top" was not installed on the presidential limousine, thereby allowing the president to have greater contact with the Dallas citizens along the motorcade route.

The president told his wife, "You sit to my left and ask Governor Connally to sit in front of us, with his wife to his left." Up front, Secret Service Agent William R. Greer was at the wheel of the presidential limousine, and Agent Roy H. Kellerman sat to his right.

The presidential motorcade departed Love Field at precisely 11:50 a.m. As was customary, a Secret Service follow-up car with eight agents trailed the presidential limousine. The responsibility of these agents was to notice suspicious individuals in crowds, activity on the roofs and in the windows of buildings along the route, and disturbances at street crossings. Two of the agents sat in the front seat of the follow-up car—a 1956 Cadillac convertible—two in the rear, and two on each running board. From time to time, two agents shifted between the follow-up car and the presidential limousine. On command or on their own initiative, the agents rode on the running boards of the follow-up car or hopped onto the rear bumper of the presidential limousine or fell back to the follow-up car.

Seated in the limousine immediately behind the follow-up car were Vice President Johnson, his wife Ladybird, and Senator Ralph W. Yarborough. The rest of the motorcade was comprised of an array of cars and buses that included various dignitaries and members of the press.

When the motorcade reached Main Street, a major thoroughfare in downtown Dallas, the president received an enthusiastic reception from the crowd.

"You see," Jacqueline said to her husband, "they really do love you here."

The motorcade was scheduled to turn right onto Houston Street and then left onto Elm Street, the most direct approach to the Trade Mart luncheon site. The Texas School Book Depository building could be seen straight ahead as the motorcade approached the intersection of Houston and Elm Street. Moving at about eleven miles per hour, the motorcade turned left onto Elm Street and began a gradual descent toward a railroad overpass on the way to the Stemmons Freeway.

Secret Service Agent Rufus W. Youngblood spotted the clock atop the Texas School Book Depository and noted that it was 12:30 p.m., exactly when the president was scheduled to arrive at the Trade Mart. One of the Secret Service agents riding with the presidential party radioed ahead to the Trade Mart to report the new estimated time of arrival. "We'll be there in about five minutes," he said.

Seconds later the sound of gunfire could be heard. The president, his hands moving to his neck, seemed to stiffen for a moment. A second or two later, Governor Connally felt a blow on his back and was thrust to his right. Mrs. Connally pulled him down onto her lap. Then another shot! This time the president was thrown violently to his left and onto the first lady's lap.

Agent Kellerman yelled at Greer, "Let's get out of here, we're hit. Get to the hospital immediately!"

Agent Clint Hill, who had been riding on the rear bumper of the presidential limousine, climbed to the aid of the first lady, who was desperately trying to rescue pieces of skull that had been blasted from the president's head. Greer put the limousine into high gear and sped off to Parkland Memorial Hospital, about four miles away.

At Parkland the president was admitted and treated immediately by a number of doctors. They noticed a faint heartbeat, although it was difficult to detect his pulse. The doctors spotted a tremendous wound on the right side of the president's head and a small round wound in the lower part of his neck. At 1:00 p.m. CST there was no heartbeat whatsoever, and the last rites were administered. At that moment John Fitzgerald Kennedy, the thirty-fifth president of the United States, was pronounced dead.

When the shots were fired, a Dallas motorcycle officer, Marrion L. Baker, riding a few cars behind the president, immediately spotted pigeons scattering from the Texas School Book Depository. He concluded that shots might have come from that area.

Baker went directly to the depository and told the building superintendent, Roy Truly, "I need to check this building." Together they went to the two elevators in the rear of the building, but both elevators were out of service and locked in place on the upper floors, so they ran up the stairs. When they reached the second floor they noticed a man walking about twenty feet away at the other end of the lunchroom. Baker asked Truly, "Who is that guy?"

Truly replied, "This man has worked here since the middle of last month." The man was identified as Lee Harvey Oswald. No more than seventy to ninety seconds had elapsed since the first shots had been heard. Within less than a minute of Oswald's encounter with Baker and Truly, Oswald passed through the second-floor offices with a Coke bottle in his hand from a vending machine in the lunchroom. At 12:40 p.m., without hurrying, Oswald left the building and boarded a bus, where he was recognized by Mrs. Mary Bledsoe, one of his former landladies. He stayed on the bus for only three to four minutes because it came to a standstill in a traffic jam. He left the bus, hailed a taxi a few blocks away, and arrived at his rooming house at 1:00 p.m.

The following events were reported by the media between November 22 and November 25, but in each instance the subsequent government inquiry into the assassination—the Warren Commission—added significant details from its many interviews of witnesses, published on September 24, 1964.

A housekeeper, Earleen Roberts, greeted Oswald and said, "I'm surprised to see you in the middle of the day." He didn't answer but started for his room. "You seem to be in quite a hurry." Just after Oswald arrived, Roberts noticed a Dallas police car stop briefly in front of her house, beep the horn a few times, and then speed off. A few minutes later Oswald left his room, zipped up his jacket; it was now between 1:04 and 1:05 p.m.

At 1:15 p.m. Patrolman J. D. Tippit of the Dallas Police Department was driving in the Oak Cliff area of Dallas, heading east on East Tenth Street, about one hundred feet past the intersection of Tenth Street and Patton Avenue. Tippit drove alongside a man walking in the same direction as his patrol car. He then stopped, got out of his car, and started to cross in front of it. The man on the sidewalk matched the general description given by the police department to Tippit, as described by a witness at the assassination site. The witness, Howard L. Brennon, observed a man shoot only once then disappear from a window of the sixth floor of the book depository. His description of the shooter was "slender white male, about 30 years old, 5 ft. 10 inches and weighing about 165–175 lbs."

The man on the sidewalk drew a gun and fired a number of shots, hitting Tippit four times and killing him. A repairman, Domingo Benavides, heard these shots and called the Dallas police on Tippit's car radio to report the incident. This message was received at 1:16 p.m.

Departing from the scene, the gunman rushed back toward Patton Avenue and made a hurried turn to the left, heading south. Helen Markham was standing on the northwest corner of Tenth Street and Patton Avenue and had seen both the killer and Tippit cross the intersection in front of her. She witnessed the shooting then saw the man with the gun in his hand walk back toward the corner and cut across the lawn of the house on the corner. He then walked south on Patton Avenue. In this same corner house, Barbara Davis and her sister-in-law, Virginia Davis, not only heard the shots but saw the man run across the lawn and shake a revolver as if to empty the used cartridges. As the gunman turned the corner, he passed alongside a taxi cab that was parked on Patton Avenue. The driver of this cab was William W. Scoggins who had seen the murder and was crouched behind his cab on the street side. After passing Scoggins, the gunman crossed to the west side of Patton Avenue and proceeded south toward Jefferson Boulevard.

On the east side of Patton Avenue, between Tenth Street and Jefferson Boulevard, used-car salesman Ted Callaway heard the shots and ran to the sidewalk. As the gunman rushed past him, Callaway shouted, "What's going on?" but the man continued to run onto Jefferson Boulevard then turned right.

The manager of the Hardy Shoe Store, Johnny Calvin Brewer, saw a man go quickly into the entrance of his store. At that same time a police car made a U-turn and headed toward the scene of the Tippit shooting. The man then left the store, but Brewer followed him. He saw him enter the Texas Theatre about sixty feet away from his shoe store and noted that this man did not buy a ticket. Brewer then said to the cashier, Julia Postal, "You know that this guy did not buy a ticket," so she called the police at about 1:40 p.m. (On the other hand, "Butch" Burroughs, the theater manager, claimed that he had sold popcorn to Oswald in the theater at 1:15 p.m. at the same time that Tippit was shot.) At 1:45 p.m. Patrolman M. N. McDonald arrived with other policemen at the movie house and ordered the man in the theater to his feet. The man was Lee Harvey Oswald. After a scuffle, the patrolman handcuffed Oswald and drove him to police headquarters.

After the assassination, police cars rushed to the Texas School Book Depository building and Inspector J. Herbert Sawyer of the Dallas Police Department arrived at the scene after hearing police radio messages at 12:34 p.m. Some of the officers assigned to that area were already interviewing witnesses and investigating the building when Sawyer arrived. Sawyer entered the building, went to the fourth floor, conducted a quick search, then returned to the main floor at 12:40 p.m. The inspector then ordered no one be permitted to leave the building. Shortly after 1:00 p.m. Capt. J. Will Fritz, chief of homicide and robbery bureau of the Dallas Police Department, took charge of the investigation. He asked Roy Truly, the building superintendent, "How many of the employees are missing at this time?"

Truly answered, "Fifteen of our people are missing." Then after forty-five minutes of further investigation, Fritz asked two detectives to pick up all the employees who at that time were missing from the building. Standing nearby were some officers who had just arrived from the Texas Theatre, where Oswald's arrest had just taken place at 1:45 pm. When Fritz mentioned the name of one missing employee, he learned that this man—Oswald—was already in custody.

One of the deputy sheriffs, Luke Mooney, was searching the sixth floor of the book depository and noticed a pile of cardboard cartons filled with books in the southeast corner. On the floor were three empty cartridge cases. One carton was placed on the floor at the side of the window so an individual could sit on it, look down Elm Street toward the overpass, and not be noticed from the outside. There was also a high stack of boxes that screened anyone at the window from others on that same sixth floor. At 1:22 p.m., about twenty minutes after the cartridge cases were found, Deputy Sheriff Eugene Boone found two rows of boxes in the northwest corner. In between the two rows of boxes was a rifle with a telescopic site. Lt. J. O'Day of the police identification bureau determined that the wooden stock and metal knob at the end of the bolt contained no fingerprints. Holding the rifle by the stock, J. Will Fritz ejected a live shell by operating the bolt. This rifle, finally determined to be a Mannlicher-Carcano, had various markings, including a serial number "C2766" as well as "1940," "Made Italy," and "CAL 6.5." The rifle was about forty inches long.

After learning of the president's death, Vice President Lyndon Baines Johnson left Parkland Hospital under close guard and went to the presidential plane that had been parked at Love Field. Jacqueline Kennedy accompanied Johnson, along with her husband's body. At 2:38 p.m. in the central compartment of the airplane, Johnson was sworn in as the thirty-sixth president of the United States by Federal District Court Judge Sarah T. Hughes. The plane then left for Washington DC, and arrived at Andrews Air Force Base in Maryland at 5:58 p.m. Eastern Standard Time.

In Dallas at about 3:00 p.m. the police arrived at the home of Ruth Paine because Lee Harvey Oswald's wife, Marina, had been staying there. The police asked Marina if her husband owned a rifle. "Yes, he does," she said. "We'd like to see it, ma'am," one of the officers asked. She led them into the garage. "There it is." She pointed to a rolled-up blanket. The officers checked the blanket but discovered no rifle there.

Throughout that day and also the next, the Dallas police held Oswald, who claimed that he was only a "patsy" and had not killed anyone. Between Friday afternoon and Sunday morning, Oswald appeared in the hallway of the police department at least sixteen times, and there was general confusion in the area. The police advised Oswald that he could communicate with an attorney, and so he made several telephone calls on Saturday trying to find an attorney. He even discussed the matter with the president of the local bar association, who offered to help find a lawyer for him. Oswald, however, declined the offer and said he would try to find counsel by himself. By Sunday morning he had made a number of phone calls to New York City and was not able to find an attorney to his liking.

At 7:10 p.m. on November 22, Oswald was formally advised that he was being charged with the murder of Patrolman J. D. Tippit. Chief of Police Jesse E. Curry brought Oswald to a press conference where many questions were shouted at Oswald and cameras were very busy taking pictures. Among this group was nightclub operator Jack Ruby, who corrected Chief Curry on the name of the organization dealing with Cuba that Oswald had formerly supported. On Saturday at 1:30 a.m. Oswald was formally charged with the assassination of President Kennedy.

On Sunday morning, November 24, Oswald was to be transferred from the city jail to the Dallas county jail, only about one mile away. An armored truck arrived shortly after 11:00 a.m. for this purpose. At 11:20 a.m. Oswald came out of the basement jail office with detectives on either side and also behind him. A man carrying a Colt .38 revolver in his right hand moved quickly to within a few feet of Oswald and fired one shot into his abdomen. Within seven minutes Oswald was at Parkland Hospital, and at 1:13 p.m. he was pronounced dead. The man who killed Oswald was Jack Ruby.

2

The Warren Commission

By Executive Order Number 11130, dated November 29, 1963, President Lyndon B. Johnson created the Commission on the Assassination of President Kennedy. The president directed this commission to evaluate all the facts and circumstances surrounding the Kennedy assassination and also the murder of alleged assassin Lee Harvey Oswald. The group was to report its findings and conclusions to Johnson.

For chairman of this commission, Johnson selected Earl Warren, the chief justice of the U.S. Supreme Court and former governor and attorney general of the state of California. From the U.S. Senate, he selected Richard B. Russell (D-GA), chairman of the Senate Armed Services Committee and a former governor of Georgia. Also from the Senate was John Sherman Cooper (R-KY), a former county and circuit judge in Kentucky and a previous U.S. ambassador to India. Two members of the commission were selected from the U.S. House of Representatives: Hale Boggs (D-LA) and Gerald R. Ford (R-MI), chairman of the House Republican Conference Committee. Johnson also chose two attorneys who had served in the administrations of both Democratic and Republican presidents. The first was Allen W. Dulles, former director of the Central Intelligence Agency, and the second was John J. McCloy, former president of the International Bank of Reconstruction and

Development, former U.S. high commissioner for Germany, and assistant secretary of war during World War II.

The composition of the quickly dubbed Warren Commission was discussed in detail by twenty-two telephone calls made by Johnson on November 25. Columnist Joseph Alsop urged the president to appoint a "special blue-ribbon panel" and avoid the unsettling prospect of Attorney General Robert F. Kennedy participating in an investigation of his brother's death. With Hale Boggs, Johnson explored the idea of a presidential commission rather than separate Senate and House investigations. The president then discussed with Speaker of the House John McCormack his intention to have regional and ideological balance. The first idea was to have two members from the Senate, two from the House, two from the judiciary, and Boggs suggested two from the public sector. This arrangement was achieved, except that the chief justice of the Supreme Court was the only representative of the judiciary. Two members were prominent Democrats (Boggs and Russell), and two were well-known Republicans (Cooper and Ford). The regional balance was achieved since three members represented the North (Ford, McCloy, and Dulles) and three were from the South (Boggs, Russell, and Cooper).

Johnson told Rep. Charles Halleck of Indiana that the assassination had significant international implications, and so he wanted members with international experience. This consideration led to the appointment of Cooper (former ambassador to India), Dulles (previous director of the CIA), and McCloy (former president of the World Bank and U.S. high commissioner for Germany). Since an assassination was involved, Johnson selected the chairman of the Armed Services Committee, Russell. From testimony of Hale Boggs's wife, Lindy, her husband was selected in part because he was one of the first to suggest to Johnson that there should be a commission. Before the assassination, Boggs had warned Kennedy not to go to Dallas because there was great infighting among the members of the Democratic Party in the state, and he did not want the president to become involved in a factional disagreement. Johnson was reluctant to appoint

Warren but later regarded it a necessity, mainly to add stature to the commission. Russell indicated that he did not want to serve, declaring that he could not serve with Warren, but Johnson later persuaded him to serve on the commission.

The commission selected the necessary staff to fulfill its assignment. J. Lee Rankin, who was former solicitor general of the United States, was sworn in as the general counsel for the commission on December 16, 1963. The commission also selected fourteen assistant counsels and an additional group that included lawyers from the Department of Justice, agents from the Internal Revenue Service, and a senior historian from the Department of Defense. Also included was an editor from the Department of State and other secretarial and administrative staff supplied by the General Services Administration and other agencies.

From November 22, 1963, a great amount of data was accumulated, especially by two of the major investigation agencies of the U.S. government, the FBI and the Secret Service, and by the commission itself. The FBI conducted approximately 25,000 interviews and re-interviews, and by September 11, 1964, there were 2,300 reports totaling approximately 25,400 pages for this commission. J. Edgar Hoover, as director of the FBI, demanded that all evidence collected in Dallas be sent to him. Also, Hoover gathered data by illegal or questionable means, including electronic bugs and illegal break-ins. All these data were sent to the "Seat of Government," SOG—Hoover's office. During the same period, the Secret Service independently conducted about 1,550 interviews and submitted 800 reports, totaling 4,600 pages. Altogether the commission and its staff took testimony from 552 witnesses. Of this latter number 94 appeared before members of the commission, 394 were questioned by members of the legal staff, 61 supplied sworn affidavits, and 3 had given various other types of statements.

On September 24, 1964, the commission presented its very lengthy report of twenty-six volumes. In chapter 1 of the report, titled "Summary and Conclusions," the commission devoted more than half of the space to what it termed Narrative of Events. In this section the commission dealt with a number of specific controversial issues. A small hole was found in the back of Kennedy's head that measured 6 x 15 mm; this was somewhat smaller than the diameter of a 6.5 mm bullet. The commission concluded that there must have been a shrinkage in the size of this opening after the bullet had passed through it. The fatal wound, however, involved the right side of Kennedy's head, and Dr. Alfred G. Olivier claimed that this wound could have been made by a bullet fired by the Mannlicher-Carcano rifle. Another small hole was located on the back 14 centimeters or 5.5 inches from the tip of the right shoulder joint, but only 7 x 4 mm in size and with very clean edges. The commission concluded that this bullet produced contusion in the upper part of the lung cavity, but no bone was struck by this bullet as it passed through Kennedy's body. The group claimed that this same bullet exited from the front part of his neck. This hole in the front of his neck was originally a small wound of 5 x 8 mm near his Adam's apple. Dallas surgeons had concluded that this was an entrance wound because of the small round edges around the wound. However, it was there that Dallas Dr. Malcolm O. Perry placed his tracheotomy in hopes of helping Kennedy with better respiration. The shirt worn by Kennedy was examined, and there was a hole 5.75 inches below the top of the collar and 1.125 inches to the right of the middle of the back of that shirt. The hole in the shirt lined up well with the bullet hole in Kennedy's back.

Governor Connally's wounds involved a bullet that entered his right shoulder, shattering his fifth rib, traveling to his wrist, but somehow exiting at his right nipple. Then this bullet punctured his left thigh. The Warren Commission concluded that all of the evidence indicated that the so-called pristine bullet later found on a stretcher in the Parkland Hospital could have caused all of his wounds. This conclusion was the only one available to the commission as long as only one gunman was involved, but three bullets were fired with two accounting for the head shot of the president and the other missing both the president and the governor.

Abraham Zapruder, a private citizen in Dallas, standing on a pedestal halfway between the underpass and the book depository, had been taking an 8 mm film of the motorcade. This film provided the most crucial and significant evidence of the Kennedy assassination. Each frame was carefully viewed to draw appropriate conclusions as to the events of November 22, 1963. Frame 225 showed Kennedy coming into view and seeming to be reacting to a neck wound by raising his hands to his throat. The commission had concluded that the bullet that had hit Kennedy in the back and exited his throat was the same bullet that struck Governor Connally. The claim was that the positions of the president and the governor were such that the same bullet probably passed through both men. This latter shot, re-ferred to as the single-bullet theory, was originally the idea of staff member, Arlen Specter, who realized that there was only one bullet to account for the wounds of the two men. This was a controversial point, especially because the bullet in Kennedy's back was later de-scribed as hitting his neck in order that it could account for the wound in the throat. Furthermore, that same bullet was found to be nearly perfect in shape, or pristine, after having caused so many wounds in both Kennedy and Connally.

As to the number of shots that were fired, the commission stated that because there were three spent cartridges found on the sixth floor of the depository, there were only three shots that were fired and one apparently missed the occupants of the limousine. Finally, the Warren Commission concluded that the three shots were fired over a period ranging from 4.8 to 7 seconds.

The Warren Commission had a great deal to say about Lee Harvey Oswald. He had purchased the rifle they claimed was used in the as-sassination, but it was ordered under the name of A. Hidell from a Chicago sporting goods company. Oswald's palm print was found on this rifle, which showed that he handled it while it was disassembled. Also, fibers found on that rifle probably had come from the shirt Os-wald was wearing on the day of the assassination. The commission found a photograph taken from Oswald's apartment showing him holding this rifle. Thus the members concluded that this weapon had been kept in his possession from the time of purchase until the day of the assassination. On Thursday, the day before the assassination, Oswald had asked a friend, Wesley Frazier, if he could ride with him to Irving, Texas, that afternoon to pick up some curtain rods for his apartment. The morning of the assassination Oswald had carried a bulky package, claiming to Frazier that it was the curtain rods. A bag of wrapping paper and tape was found on the southeast corner of the sixth floor of the depository, alongside the window that the commission claimed was the position of the assassin. Oswald used this wrapping paper, the commission claimed, to carry his rifle to work. The commission further determined that four of Oswald's prints were left on two boxes near the window on the sixth floor of the depository and also on the paper sack found in that same area.

Witnesses to the assassination were interviewed, but the one who gave the most complete description was Howard Brennon. He described a slender white male in his early thirties about 165 to 175 pounds. But he was 120 feet away from the sixth-floor window of the book depository. His final claim, according to the commission, was that he saw a man in the window who closely resembled Oswald.

The commission then drew twelve major conclusions, incorporating many of the specific issues just enumerated. It found that all the shots were fired from the Texas School Book Depository because no evidence was found that any shots had come from anywhere else. This conclusion, according to the commission, was based on eight points. Witnesses at the scene of the assassination claimed they saw a rifle being fired from the sixth-floor window of the depository building. On this same floor a Mannlicher-Carcano rifle was found from which was fired the nearly whole bullet that appeared supposedly on Governor Connally's stretcher at Parkland Memorial Hospital. In addition, two bullet fragments were found in the front seat of the presidential limousine. Also from this rifle were the three used cartridge cases found near the window of the southeast corner of that sixth floor. A bullet fragment from this same rifle struck the windshield of the presidential limousine on the inside surface of the glass that was not penetrated. The nature of the bullet wounds suffered by both President Kennedy and Governor Connally and the location of the car at the time of the shots established that the bullets were fired from above and behind the presidential limousine. President Kennedy was struck by a bullet that entered the back of his neck, exiting in the lower portion of his neck, and then was struck a second time by a bullet that entered the right part of his head, causing a massive wound. Governor Connally was struck by a bullet that entered the right side of his back, traveling downward through the right side of his chest, passing through his right wrist, and finally entering the left thigh. There was no evidence that shots were fired from the triple underpass ahead of the motorcade or from any other location. All of these points led to the first conclusion that all shots came from the Texas School Book Depository.

Two bullet fragments were found in the front seat; one likely came from a nose portion of a bullet and the other from the base portion of a bullet. Three other lead particles were on the rug beneath the jump seat where Nellie Connally was sitting. And some small cracks appeared in the outer layer of the windshield along with a dent in the strip of chrome across the top of the windshield. Robert A. Frazier, an expert from the FBI, claimed that the dent in the chrome on the windshield was caused by a projectile that struck it on the inside surface. Thus these fragments indicated that one bullet missed both Kennedy and Connally.

According to the commission, book cartons were piled up to five feet high in front of a window in the southeast corner of the sixth floor of the book depository, and three empty cartridge cases were discovered near this window. These three cartridge cases led to the second major conclusion that only three shots were fired.

Connally was brought into trauma room number 2 of Parkland Hospital and then taken by elevator to the second-floor operating room. He was then transferred from a stretcher to the operating-room table, and a hospital attendant wheeled the stretcher into an elevator. Shortly after that, Darryl C. Tomlinson, a senior engineer at the hospital, took this stretcher from the elevator and placed it in the corridor on the ground floor, alongside another stretcher that was likely not connected with the governor's care. A few minutes later Tomlinson bumped one of these stretchers against the wall, and to his surprise, a bullet rolled out. The commission concluded that this bullet had come from the governor's stretcher. This same bullet was the pristine bullet, one of the three shots described in the second conclusion.

Although the commission recognized that Governor Connally strongly believed that he was not hit by the same bullet that first struck President Kennedy, their third conclusion was that all the shots that caused the governor's wounds were also fired from the sixth-floor window of the book depository. Connally testified before the commission and felt certain that he heard the first shot, turned to look behind himself, and then one to one-half seconds later felt a bullet strike his right shoulder. The time between the sound of the bullet and the feeling of a bullet striking him convinced the governor that one bullet could not explain the two events.

The Warren Commission then dealt with Lee Harvey Oswald and determined that the following points were true. The Mannlicher-Carcano 6.5 mm Italian rifle from which the shots were fired was owned by Oswald, who carried this rifle into the depository building on the morning of the assassination. At the time of the assassination Oswald was at the window where the shots were fired, and shortly after the assassination, this rifle was found hidden between cartons on the sixth floor. In addition, a paper bag that Oswald had brought to the depository was also discovered near the window where the shots were fired. Based on the testimony of experts, the commission concluded that Oswald had the capability to fire the shots from that rifle within the elapsed time of the shooting. Finally, Oswald had lied to the police after his arrest on various matters and earlier, on April 10, 1963, had tried to assassinate Maj. Gen. Edwin A. Walker. This attempt demonstrated his predisposition to take a human life. From

these seven points the commission arrived at its fourth conclusion—
that the shots that killed President Kennedy and wounded Governor
Connally were all fired by Oswald.

The commission then directed its attention to Oswald's alleged
contact with Patrolman J. D. Tippit and made the following determi-
nations. Two eyewitnesses saw the Tippit shooting, seven heard the
shots and saw the gunman leave the scene with his revolver, and nine
positively identified Oswald as the man they saw. The cartridge cases
found at the scene of the Tippit shooting were fired from the revolver
in Oswald's possession at the time of his arrest, and this revolver was
bought by and belonged to him. Lastly, Oswald's jacket was found
along the path taken by him as he fled from the scene of the Tippit
killing. These four points led the commission to its fifth conclusion—
that Oswald killed Tippit about forty-five minutes after the president's
assassination.

The sixth conclusion was that within eighty minutes of the assassination and thirty-five minutes of the Tippit killing, Oswald had re-
sisted arrest at the movie theater, where he tried to shoot another
police officer.

Oswald's detention by the Dallas police was the point of concern
that led to the seventh conclusion by the Warren Commission. Except
for the force that was required at his arrest, Oswald was not physically
coerced by any law-enforcement officials. All media reporters were permitted access to the area where Oswald was allowed to pass when he
was moved from his cell to the interrogation room and other parts of
the building. These movements created chaotic, confused conditions
and were not conducive to an orderly interrogation and the protection
of his rights. Finally, the numerous statements made by the press during all this confusion and disorder at the police station could have presented some clear obstacles in obtaining a fair trial for Oswald.

The Warren Commission then directed its attention to Jack Ruby
and his final contact with Oswald. They determined that Ruby entered the basement of the Dallas Police Department shortly after
11:17 a.m. on November 24 and shot Oswald at 11:21 a.m. Although

there were questions as to how Ruby gained entry to that area, the evidence is that he walked down a ramp leading from Main Street to the basement of the police department building. There was no evidence that Ruby was assisted by any members of the Dallas Police Department in killing Oswald, and finally, the decision to transfer Oswald to the county jail in full public view was unsound. These latter points led to the obvious eighth conclusion, viewed on television by millions of Americans, that Oswald was killed by Ruby on November 24.

The commission was concerned about whether or not there was any evidence of a conspiracy to kill Kennedy. Their points on this question were numerous. The members found no evidence that anyone had helped Oswald to plan or carry out the assassination and that he was not involved with any person, political group, or foreign government in a conspiracy to assassinate the president. There was no more than speculation that Oswald was a part of the FBI or the CIA. The commission discovered no relationship between Oswald and Ruby, who had acted alone in killing Oswald. Finally there was no evidence that Tippit knew Ruby or Oswald. All of these points led the commission to the ninth conclusion: there was no evidence that either Oswald or Ruby was part of any conspiracy to assassinate President Kennedy.

The tenth conclusion from the commission was that there was no conspiracy or disloyalty to the U.S. government by any federal, state, or local official.

One of the final points dealt with the personality and character of Oswald. The Warren group considered his resentment of all authority, his inability to enter into any meaningful relationships with others, and his urge to try to find a place in history despite his past failures. In addition, they noted his capacity for violence, as indicated by his attempt to assassinate Walker and his commitment to Marxism and Communism. From these considerations the eleventh conclusion of the commission was that Oswald acted alone in assassinating President Kennedy.

Members of the commission understood the responsibilities of the president to make frequent trips to all parts of the United States and abroad, as a twelfth conclusion. They recognized these trips as complexities of the presidency that had increased in recent years so that the Secret Service was not able to maintain complete security around the president.

3

Scanty Evidence for the Warren Commission Conclusions

THE FIRST CONCLUSION OF the Warren Commission was that all bullets had come from the Texas School Book Depository Building. One witness, S. M. Holland, had claimed that he heard four shots and one sounded as though it had come, not from behind the motorcade, but from the trees on the north side of Elm Street, where he saw a puff of smoke. This evidence argues for a shot coming from the grassy knoll. A major point in this book is the sudden slamming of Kennedy's body to his left, strongly arguing for a bullet from the grassy knoll.

When the shots were fired there were many individuals around the book depository who believed that shots had come from the railroad bridge over the triple underpass in front of the motorcade. Many spectators ran in the direction of this triple underpass, running toward where they thought the shots had originated while others fled from that scene. Patrolman J. W. Foster of the Dallas Police Department counted ten or eleven people on this railroad bridge, and other witnesses judged the number to be between fourteen and eighteen. Finally, it was decided by the police that there were fifteen people on the railroad bridge. Foster claimed that he had checked the credentials of those individuals who were on this bridge.

FBI Special Agent Winston G. Lawson motioned through the

windshield of the lead car of the motorcade for Foster to get the people on the bridge away from the position directly in the path of the motorcade. This directive was unsuccessful, and those people did not move, but there was no clear evidence that shots came from the bridge.

However, physical evidence on Kennedy's body provides other evidence. There was the small round hole in the front of Kennedy's neck, near his Adam's apple, that Dallas surgeons believed was an entrance wound because of its size. Generally, exit wounds are irregular and much larger than entrance wounds, and the size and regularity of this hole indicated to the surgeons at the Parkland Hospital that it was likely an entrance wound. Since a tracheotomy was done at this same area, later autopsy findings could not verify the original size and shape of this wound.

Personnel at the Army Wounds Ballistics Laboratory at the Edgewood Arsenal in Maryland examined this question and fired bullets from the rifle recovered at the book depository at a distance of 180 feet. These bullets were shot through an animal skin, and the entry site showed, as expected, holes that were very regular and round. On the exit side the holes were elongated, indicating that the bullet had become unstable at the point of exit.

The Warren Commission concluded that a bullet entered the president's back then went through his entire body and exited at the Adam's apple area. But it would be quite amazing if the round and small hole seen by the Dallas surgeons was an exit area. If the throat wound was, in fact, an entrance wound, a shot in front of the president from the railroad bridge seems unlikely, because Patrolman Foster seemed certain that the fifteen people there had appropriate credentials. The only other place for such a hidden shooter, placed in front of the president's car, is from an opened manhole cover leading to a storm drain at the bottom of the grassy knoll, mentioned in the 1992 tapes *The Men Who Killed Kennedy* (Central TV Enterprise). Reenactment showed that it would have taken a shooter hiding under the manhole cover twenty minutes to escape through the tunnels to the Trinity River.

Perhaps a more significant matter is whether or not one could conceive of a bullet coming downward from six floors and then taking an upward course. The bullet entered the back area around the second or third thoracic (T2-T3) vertebra, which was 5.75 inches from the top of the president's collar, without hitting any bone and then supposedly exiting from the Adam's apple area. One can see how low that bullet would have entered, measuring 5.75 inches down from a collar, and easily see how unlikely it would be for that same bullet to have exited around the Adam's apple area.

Clearly, autopsy surgeons were unable to find any path for that bullet entering the president's back into any of the large muscles in the back of the neck. Also, one of these autopsy surgeons, U.S. Army Lt. Col. Pierre Finck, could not track the bullet hole in the back for more than the tip of his finger. In order to explain how one bullet could cause injuries to both the back and the neck, the Warren Commission hypothesized that this bullet found its way between two large muscles in the neck without leaving any evidence of damage and then emerged out of the throat area. This is just one of the major problems with the conclusions of the Warren Commission. It tried to sell the idea that a shot came from the sixth floor of the depository, traveled in a downward direction, entered nearly six inches below the collar, and left a track that could only be viewed as a fingertip in length, then made its way, without hitting any bony structures, in an upward direction so that it could come out of the Adam's apple area.

In a recent book *Passion for Truth*, Senator Arlen Specter, author of the single-bullet theory, states, "The entrance wound on the neck was about an inch below the shoulder line in the president's back" (page 88). The latter statement makes sense only if one assumes Specter is so committed to his single-bullet theory that he refers to the back as the neck in order to allow for an exit in the throat. Another member of the commission, Gerald Ford, was originally responsible for the change in wording from *back* to *neck* to allow for the bullet hole in the throat to be from a single bullet.

An even more incredible idea is that this bullet then struck

Governor Connally, who was not sitting in a position that it could easily hit his right armpit. The bullet then proceeded through his right
chest, piercing the right lung, which then collapsed. The bullet supposedly emerged at the right nipple and continued through the governor's right wrist, shattering the distal end of the radius bone of the
arm, partially severing his radial nerve, and then eventually came to
rest in his left thigh. This is what is proposed by the single-bullet theory. Even more incredible is that this single bullet came the whole way
through the president and then also through the governor and survived in a nearly pristine or perfect shape.

Specter claims that the weight of the pristine bullet was 158.6
grains, but this type of bullet usually weighs 160 grains, allowing for
only 1.4 grains to be left in Connally's body. Tolerance for the original
weight, however, may well be beyond 1.4 grains, and so no conclusion
can be drawn from these facts. On the other hand, nurse Audrey Bell
collected five separate bullet fragments taken from Connally's body,
and these could not be part of the pristine bullet. This evidence is very
strong and argues that the pristine bullet could not have gone through
both Kennedy and Connally, but requires that another bullet struck
Connally. After all, the governor testified that he was certain he was
hit by a bullet after the president was struck, while he was responding
to the sound of a gunshot and turning to see what had happened to
the president. The one and one-half seconds between the sound of the
first shot and Connally's reaction to his wound is too short a time to
assume that a lone shooter could reload and fire a second time. The re-
quirement by the single-bullet theorists that this one bullet went
through both Kennedy and Connally has completely failed.

One of the major criticisms of the Warren Commission deals with
the enormous cavity on the right side of Kennedy's head due to trau-
matic removal of the right part of his brain. Dallas Dr. Robert McClelland had stated that almost 25 percent of the president's brain was
missing. The commission indicated that there was absence of scalp
and bone as well, producing a defect that measured about 5.25 inches
in its greatest diameter. One can see how large this defect would be,

but viewing the photos said to be the president's head during the autopsy, at least one of them shows a continuous amount of hair covering that right side, with only a tiny hole at the back of the head. This type of picture is inconceivable when one reads that there was absence of scalp and bone for a defect of 5.25 inches from one tip to the other. Furthermore, the major blood-containing cavity (sinus) in the middle of the head, between the two major hemispheres, was very much torn and disrupted. Major fracture lines of the skull varied in length, but the longest measured 19 centimeters or 7.5 inches. When viewing the cleaned-up version of the Zapruder film, one is most impressed by the exploding of the right hemisphere with a cloud of brain and blood that blurs the picture at the moment the missile strikes the right side of the president's head. Three fragments of skull bone were recovered; x-rays showed small particles of metal in these fragments. Other x-rays of the skull revealed many different minute, metallic fragments in the remaining right cerebral cortex, that is, the superficial portion of the brain on the right side. All of these major changes can not be explained by a single intact bullet.

One of the major points we make in this book is that a bullet making only a tiny hole in the soft tissue of the back and tracked for only the length of a finger tip is not at all the same type of bullet that can splatter nearly the whole right hemisphere of Kennedy's head. These must be different bullets from different guns. The latter is called a frangible bullet that can produce such enormous amounts of damage and also produce metallic fragments, not only in the pieces of bone that were scattered, even to the rear of the car, but also in the remaining skull bone and finally in the remaining brain that was not blasted away by this same bullet. One cannot assume that a given gun with a given type of bullet could produce, on the one hand, such a tiny hole in the back and, on the other hand, such an enormous amount of destruction as to remove the right side of the president's head. There must have been at least two different kinds of guns and two different types of bullets in order to account for this enormous difference between the effects of the bullet in the back and the bullet in the head.

A supplemental report of the autopsy, done at the Naval Medical Center in Bethesda, Maryland, was prepared by Drs. James J. Humes and J. Thornton Boswell, who had left medical practice for largely administrative positions. They indicated that the laceration of the right hemisphere extended from the tip of the occipital lobe, which is the very back of the head, the entire way to the tip of the frontal lobe, which is the most anterior part of the brain. The extension of this entire blast lesion also involved the corpus callosum. This structure is in the middle of the brain and ties together the two hemispheres, and in this instance, the president's corpus callosum was lacerated from its head to its tail. Even the left side of the brain was involved by the marked congestion or engorgement of blood vessels of the left temporal (above ear) and frontal regions. The base of the brain, called the brain stem, was not spared, and there were torn areas in the midbrain from the floor of it to a cavity deep in the brain, so that the very depths of the brain were also significantly damaged.

Let us now explore the possibility that Lee Harvey Oswald was, in fact, involved in this assassination. First, the commission had decided that Oswald had brought his rifle to work on the morning of the assassination. Oswald had claimed that he was going to carry some curtain rods to work that morning. and he told this to his neighbor, Buell Frazier. Frazier's sister, Linnie Mae Randle, saw him carrying this package and estimated it to be about twenty-eight inches long; Frazier himself thought that it was around twenty-four inches long. This rifle, however, when disassembled, was almost forty inches long, so the length of the package is important. The best estimates of Frazier and his sister was that this package was not long enough to be the disassembled rifle. According to Frazier and Randle, Oswald carried this package under his armpit, extending to his hand, and his arm length was not forty inches, but more like twenty-four inches.

And what of the wrapping paper that supposedly was used to carry the curtain rods? It is true that some of Oswald's prints were on it, but that doesn't prove that this was the paper bag that had the rifle inside. As for the cardboard cartons near the window where the rifle was found, it is not surprising that some prints of Oswald's were on these cartons. There is no indication whatsoever when these prints were placed there. After all, he worked on the sixth floor, and his prints should be there.

Eyewitness accounts of the figure on the sixth floor, including the testimony of Howard Brennon, wavered from time to time as to whether or not a positive identification could be made. Three additional witnesses were not able to clearly identify who was standing at that window. What of Marrion L. Baker, the motorcycle cop who entered the depository somewhere between seventy to ninety seconds after the first shot? Tests have been run to show that, at a normal walking speed, it took about seventy-eight seconds to move from the southeast corner of the sixth floor to the second-floor lunchroom. And the elevators were locked up. Baker did not report that Oswald was out of breath. The amount of time it would have taken Oswald to go from the sixth floor to the second was such that it is very questionable that he would have had time to be on the second floor in such a relaxed state. Thus, it is unlikely that Oswald could have been a shooter on the sixth floor and still encounter Baker seventy to ninety seconds later on the second floor.

A major controversy surrounds the question of whether or not Oswald was such an outstanding marksman that he could have hit the target under the circumstances of the assassination. In the marines, Oswald was described as only a "fairly good shot," and in his last recorded test was said to be a "rather poor shot." It is important to know that, when Oswald went to Russia, he joined a hunting club, and he was considered such a poor shot that other members felt sorry for him. He could never hit anything. His friends often gave him some of the game they had killed since he had missed most of his own shots. The Warren Commission concluded that Oswald had fired three shots with two hits during a span of 4.8 to 5.6 seconds. Expert riflemen could not fire the assassination weapon quite that fast, because it required a minimum time of 2.25 seconds between shots. Thus one must conclude that Oswald would probably not have been capable of firing that many shots in such a short period of time, nor was he an outstanding marksman.

Dallas Police Officer J. D. Tippit was killed by someone at 1:15 p.m., and the news of his death was sent to the police at 1:16 p.m. Remember that Oswald left his rooming house (without a car) at 1:05–6 p.m., ten minutes prior to Tippit's murder. The distance from the rooming house to where Tippit was killed was nine-tenths of a mile. Calculations show that a person would have to walk at the pace of 5.4 miles per hour to have gone that distance within that ten-minute period. In the walking world even an advanced walker can do 4.0–4.1 miles per hour. At this speed such an individual would have to be in excellent shape, working out five or six times a week for at least six months to maintain that walking speed. Therefore, it seems unlikely that there would have been enough time for Oswald to have arrived at the Tippit murder scene.

Helen Markham, a witness to the Tippit killing, was able to pick Oswald out of a lineup, but she was hysterical at the time and claimed that the killer was a heavy man. Her description of the clothes worn by the killer was very different from witness Ted Callaway. Another witness (Acquilla Clemons) said there were two men, not one, attacking Tippit. There were four lineups, and in each, the others in the lineup were significantly different from Oswald in dress and stature. Some witnesses claimed the killer ran east and others said west on Tenth Street. Furthermore, Tippit was shot with an automatic pistol; Oswald had a revolver. The shell casings are different for these two weapons. Do note that it was Oswald who appeared in front of the shoe store and then went into the Texas Theatre. No one is certain of his whereabouts between the time he left his rooming house and the time he appeared near the shoe store.

Finally, Arlen Specter, in his recent book *Passion for Truth,* writes with brutal frankness about the behavior of the commissioners whom he witnessed as part of that group. On page 84 he states, "Allen Dulles may have withheld vital information from the commission, the type of vital information we were counting on him to supply." Specter also noted that Chief Justice Earl Warren played a heavy hand in suppressing evidence and steering the commission away from sensitive matters. Hoover and the FBI stonewalled and misled the commission, Specter claimed, and he actually blamed the group for giving rise to the conspiracy theories. In addition, attendance at the six hundred interviews held by the commission over a seven-and-a-half-month period were 2 percent (Richard B. Russell), 8 percent (John J. McCloy), 10 percent (Hale Boggs), 15 percent (John S. Cooper), 18 percent (Dulles), 20 percent (Gerald R. Ford), and 22 percent (Warren). On the average, their attendance was only one out of every seven interviews. At times, the commissioners departed after the beginning of the interview, and thus, the attendance figures are maximal values.

In summary, one can see that it is nearly inconceivable that the major conclusions of the Warren Commission were correct. There are many reasons to reject nearly every finding. Other specific reasons will be clarified in the next chapter. Finally, after all of the hundreds of witnesses and thousands of pages of transcript, one cannot help but wonder how the commission could have failed to expose the truth. One major point here is that the Warren Commission accepted the evidence implicating the lone gunman, Oswald, and disregarded any evidence indicating a conspiracy. In the twenty-first century there are many historians who truly believe the commission felt committed to conclude that only a lone gunman was involved because the American people could not handle the idea that there were many forces that came together as a conspiracy to assassinate President John F. Kennedy.

4

Insights into the Assassination

Oliver Stone

Some have seen Oliver Stone's *JFK* many times, and each time any viewer with knowledge of the facts in evidence will be impressed by how accurate many of the scenes are in that movie. Stone and his movie, however, have often been trashed by the media. It is clear that many in the media are not in favor of any conspiracy theory of the Kennedy assassination. The media seem content to promote the lone-gunman theory, involving Lee Harvey Oswald, and the single-bullet theory, involving one bullet going through both the president and Governor Connally.

The scene is the National Press Club in Washington DC, and the time is January 15, 1992. The organization invited Stone to speak before the members and also a nationwide audience on C-SPAN television. Although no book resulted from his speech, a transcription is available. The president of the NPC, Katherine Kahler, asked Stone to clarify the frequently asked question, "Does the Deep Throat Man X character, played by Donald Sutherland, really exist?"

Stone responded, "I'm very glad you asked this because so many people have asked me when they came out of the movie, who is man

X? Let me just say that man X exists. He's here today on the podium. He is Fletcher Prouty. He served in the military since before World War II. From 1955 to 1964 he was in the Pentagon, working as chief of special operations with the Joint Chiefs of Staff during the Kennedy years. He is responsible for providing the military support of the clandestine operations of the CIA, the so-called black operations."

Prouty is an important individual when considering any conspiracy theory. He is important because he writes about his personal experiences in the Kennedy assassination and therefore has firsthand information. Stone made some additional comments about Prouty, that he served his country well, retired as a full colonel, and has written a number of books, including *Secret Team*. Prouty had been critical of the CIA's illegitimate activities, particularly in the 1950s and 1960s. He knew a great deal about some important individuals who were related to the assassination, like Allen Dulles, head of the CIA, and Gen. Charles Cabell, also of the CIA. Prouty understood the atmosphere at the Pentagon and the CIA at that time and retired in 1964 from the Pentagon and later becoming a banker.

Stone makes the point that the lone-gunman theory proposed by the Warren Commission in its twenty-six volumes is not believed by the majority of Americans. He asks various questions of what we are to believe based on the commission's findings. First is that Oswald supposedly used a mail-order Italian rifle, dubbed by the Italian army the "humanitarian rifle," because it rarely killed anyone when deliberately aimed. Then are we to believe that a high-school dropout from Fort Worth, Texas, who professed Marxism, was taken to a secret marine base in Japan where the U2 flights originated, given courses in Russian, and then permitted to leave the corps with three days' notice on a trumped-up claim of a mother's illness? Next, are we to believe that Oswald went to the U.S. Embassy in Moscow and announced his intention to defect and turn over U.S. secrets to the Russians and was then permitted to go on his way? Are we also to believe that this same individual, eighteen months later, came to the same U.S. Embassy, announced his intention to resume his American citizenship, and was handed a passport and funds to allow him to return home?

Stone questioned, Are we to believe that he was met by a CIA representative on his return to the United States but never debriefed, although thousands of tourists that same year were so debriefed? The next question was how Patrolman Marrion Baker, at around seventy to ninety seconds after the beginning of the shooting, found Oswald on the second floor with a Coca-Cola and showing no signs of being out of breath? Other questions are the stashing of this rifle without any obvious handprints and the three cartridges laid side by side at the window on the sixth floor. Finally, there's the issue of Oswald's cool, calm behavior that weekend, claiming that he was a patsy. One of the last questions asked by Stone is about Allen Dulles, who had been fired by Kennedy as director of the CIA as part of the president's aim to splinter this agency. Why was this same man appointed to the Warren Commission to investigate Kennedy's murder?

Next, Stone challenges the absurd single-bullet theory. This bullet broke two dense bones and came out as a nearly pristine bullet. The bullet supposedly entered Kennedy's back on a downward trajectory but then changed its direction, exiting through his throat, paused for about 1.6 seconds, then struck Governor Connally. The bullet then turned right, then left, then right again as it hit Connally in the back of the right armpit. Next it headed downward, through his chest, took a right turn at his wrist, shattered the radius bone, and exited. The bullet then seemed to take a U-turn and bury itself in Connally's left thigh. This same bullet turned up in pristine condition five miles from the scene of this crime, in the corridor of Parkland Hospital. It is incredible that a generation of journalists and historians have refused to carefully examine most of these questions and have closed ranks to criticize those who have analyzed the facts.

The final point of Stone's discussion is the motivation behind the assassination. The important question was whether Kennedy was planning to withdraw from Vietnam. Did this make a difference to the military-industrial complex? Prouty was one of the authors of

Kennedy's National Security Action Memo (NSAM) No. 263 of October 11, 1963, which announced his plan to have one thousand military advisers home for Christmas and to have all U.S. personnel out of Vietnam by the end of 1965. Historian Arthur Schlesinger Jr., who was closely associated with Kennedy, reported on the president's intention to withdraw from Vietnam. Such a withdrawal would have meant that the corporations providing the war machine in Vietnam would find their profits disappearing.

Stone's final comment was a call for the opening of the Kennedy files before the stated year of 2029. Many Americans have wondered why these files have to be sealed until that late date—unless there is some good reason to hide certain facts. Despite frequent requests that these closed files be available before 2029, no one has yet managed to accomplish this task.

Dr. Cyril Wecht

DR. CYRIL WECHT served as coroner for Allegheny County, Pennsylvania, for many years and has been an outstanding member in various editorial positions on the boards of medical and legal publications. He has also written extensively about such matters. Wecht testified before the U.S. House of Representatives' Committee on Assassinations, with Robert Blakey as chief counsel and staff director. The transcript of his testimony is available for commentary.

One important question was whether or not a bullet could indeed strike a rib and a radius bone of a human being and emerge as a pristine bullet. Considering that this same bullet had supposedly gone through both the president and the governor, Wecht claims that no bullet could have caused all the wounds of these two men and emerged pristine. The problem is the positioning of the two men, and Wecht believes that Governor Connally would have had to move a foot or more to the left and back or the president would have had to lean almost out of the car and then come back to his position for the bullet to have gone through both men according to the single-bullet theory.

Coming out of the sixth-floor window, this bullet was moving downward at an angle of 20 to 25 degrees, striking the president in the back, then taking an upward direction and coming out of the president's Adam's apple, and hitting Governor Connally with a 25-degree angle of another course. It would have to make an acute angular turn and come back almost two feet, stop, and make a second turn before it hit the governor behind his right armpit. This bullet then fractured the radius bone of Connally, who was six foot four, a large man, and therefore with heavy bones. The same bullet had pulverized five inches of his right fifth rib, and we are to believe that such a bullet would arrive in a pristine condition after doing all of that damage? This same bullet would have to have hit the governor's radial nerve, which was partially severed at a time when he was still holding his hat. In order to hold his hat, his radial nerve would have to be intact. He could not have held onto his hat as long as he did if the single-bullet theory were correct. Thus, this is further evidence against the timing of the one bullet that had already gone through the president to have also gone through the governor.

Wecht then refers to a bullet that was fired into cotton wadding, striking nothing and coming to rest in that soft material. He noted that this bullet showed more deformity than the pristine bullet that presumably went through both the president and the governor, shattering certain bones.

During the committee hearings Wecht was questioned not only about the bullet in the back but about a possible second bullet that hit the president's head, a bullet in addition to the one that hit the rear of Kennedy's head. Wecht mentioned the very important point that this second bullet into the head would have to be frangible ammunition because of the tremendous deformity of the scalp and the bone. He concluded there was a real possibility of a second shot that struck the president in the head, synchronized to the bullet that hit the back of the head. He was asked whether this bullet may have come from the side (the grassy knoll), and Wecht indicated that it was a possibility. Finally, Wecht indicated he believed another bullet missed the car entirely, and therefore, at least four shots were fired, two hitting Kennedy, one hitting Connally, and one missing both men. Could four shots have been fired by a lone gunman? This seems to be out of the question. Wecht was asked about the bullet that went into Kennedy's back. He believed it may have been fired from a lower floor of the Texas School Book Depository building, therefore raising again the likelihood there was more than one gunman in the building.

A final question was asked about what had happened to President Kennedy's brain, an important organ to examine in order to get some definite answers to many of the questions posed in this investigation. After the autopsy, the brain was placed into the security of Dr. George Burkley, the White House physician, and then guarded by Secret Service Agent Roy H. Kellerman and finally given to Robert Bouck, head of the protective research division of the Secret Service in 1963. On April 22, 1965, Robert F. Kennedy authorized the release of this material to Evelyn Lincoln, who had been President Kennedy's secretary but who also had an office in the National Archives. Included in these materials was a stainless-steel container, seven by eight inches, which probably contained the president's brain. On October 31, 1966, Burke Marshall, representing the Kennedy family, transferred this material to the National Archives, but there was no steel container in these holdings. Robert F. Kennedy had expressed concern that these materials, especially the brain, might be placed on public display, and he wanted to prevent that. Although there is no proof, it seems probable that the president's brother is likely responsible for the absence of the president's brain.

Wecht suggests there is a formidable obstacle of a political nature that seems to prevent people from looking objectively at the Kennedy assassination. The moment one abandons the single-bullet theory is the moment one has to consider at least two people were involved in the shooting, and that means there was a criminal conspiracy. And this seems to be a step some individuals cannot consider. This concept of political assassination suggests a political takeover and it cannot be considered by some individuals in this country, especially those in the media. Recent polls, however, show that at least 85 percent of Americans believe that only a wide-ranging conspiracy might explain the assassination.

THE THEORIES by Oliver Stone and Cyril Wecht are emphasized here because they have both focused in a clear and succinct way on the crucial features of the Warren Commission that were basically incorrect. They do not go far enough, however, because they mainly criticize what is wrong with the Warren Commission's report. They show what did not happen rather than what did happen.

There are two other individuals who have excellent descriptions of the important details around this assassination. The first is Robert Groden, author of *The Search for Lee Harvey Oswald: A Comprehensive Photographic Record.* This book is an excellent photographic atlas with pictures of all who were connected to this assassination. He provides details about Rose Cheramie, the individual who warned that Kennedy would be killed in late November. Groden's account of Oswald's alleged trip to Mexico City is excellent, likely dealing with a double of Oswald, another meeting involving a so-called Leon Oswald, and the other examples of the prediction that Kennedy would be killed in November. Groden has a complete story about Oswald and his earlier life and all the conditions around the shooting of the president and J. D. Tippit. Finally, Groden accounts well for all the many bullets that were fired during the assassination, and of course, there were more than three.

The other individual who needs to be singled out (again) is Col. Fletcher Prouty. In all of the books written about the assassination, there are few offering a convincing firsthand evidence of the events surrounding the assassination, except for the accounts from Prouty. He was an outstanding military man who was the only one in this epic to relate his firsthand information. He spells out the conditions behind the TFX fighter plane (which became the F111) and the awards that were given based on political, not military, considerations. This political award obviously angered many of the military-industrial complex and also the air force. He was there to explain National Security Action Memo No. 55, which essentially removed the CIA from the cold war and therefore downgraded that agency. He was there and knew a great deal about the NSAM No. 263 and the indications that Kennedy planned to pull out of Vietnam. There is no question of what that would have done to the war machine that provided the military equipment, and it would have had a major effect on the military-industrial complex. Finally, of great import is his account that he was sent to Antarctica at the time of the assassination and therefore would be out of the loop in trying to protect the president in Dallas. Prouty was, of course, Mr. X in the very well-known movie *JFK* and explained the essentials of the conspiracy theory in that movie. It is extremely unlikely that this outstanding military man could have fabricated the whole story or lied in his description of the conspiracy that was developing at that time. We must pay close attention to the only firsthand evidence we have about the forces that were very real at the time of Kennedy's assassination. Furthermore, it was Prouty who claimed that a Texan military unit should have been directed to help with security. One was standing by, but it was not finally requested. He also points out that the Secret Service had no one on foot in Dealey Plaza. The night before the assassination the Secret Service group was in a tavern, The Cellar, until the early morning of November 22.

Other books that have made contributions are *Crossfire* by James Marrs, who has written a comprehensive account of the conspiracy theory that included many interviews of the primary witnesses. Another book, *The Killing of the President* by Robert Groden, offers the special feature of photographs of individuals and places involved in the crime. Anthony Summer's *Not in Your Lifetime* is an honest investigation of many witnesses and their stories, with an emphasis on Oswald and his time in New Orleans in 1963. *High Treason* by Harrison Livingstone and Robert Groden provides an excellent account of the medical evidence. Finally, Peter Dale Scott has written an insightful book on *Deep Politics and the Death of JFK,* emphasizing the corruption of American politics that set the scene for the assassination. Mark

Lane's *Rush to Judgment* has thoroughly investigated certain aspects of the assassination, especially the rifle that Oswald supposedly used. One other book that should be mentioned is *Case Closed* by the very clever Gerald Posner, a darling of the media, who, like the Warren Commission, chooses the facts that support the lone-gunman and single-bullet theories and disregards the points that don't fit, concluding that no conspiracy took place.

Most of the information given in the books written about the assassination, including those described above, have emphasized what did not happen, but in the following chapters we are going to explain what actually did happen.

5

The Giancana
Connection

IT IS NOW TWELVE years later—1975. The most important character in
the event about to take place is Sam Giancana, at onetime top Mafia
boss in Chicago and still an important crime syndicate figure.

Some of the players in the Kennedy killing will be involved in this
next event, and we will explore the forces that could tie these two
men together. The first is the CIA. After the Bay of Pigs invasion by
anti-Castro forces on April 16, 1961, Kennedy fired the leaders of the
CIA and blamed them rather than himself for this disaster. In 1963 it
was get-even time against the president for some dissidents in the
CIA, who were spotted in Dallas on November 22 at the time of the
killing. Next is the FBI. J. Edgar Hoover, director of the FBI, hated
Kennedy and was motivated to contribute to his demise. Also, he established the Top Hoodlum Program to target the Mafia, especially
leaders like Giancana. Thus these two governmental organizations
could link these two men together. The third force is the Mafia itself.
Its leaders had strong motivations to kill Kennedy.

The date is June 19, 1975. A Senate investigating committee,
chaired by Senator Frank Church (D-IA), is carefully checking into all
the CIA's dirty tricks, especially the assassination of heads of state. One
of these dates back to 1961, when Sam Giancana, boss of the Chicago

Mafia and probably the most powerful mobster in the nation at the time, headed a team put together by the CIA to kill Fidel Castro. Although the CIA was implicated in eliminating four other heads of state—the Dominican Republic's Rafael Trujillo, South Vietnam's Ngo Dinh Diem, Congo's Patrice Lumumba, and Chile's Rene Schneider—it was embarrassed that Castro survived. Later, in chapter eight, we will show that Giancana's team did not take seriously the plot to kill Castro and made only token efforts to do so. The CIA's greatest embarrassment was, however, that a Senate committee was finding out all about their dirty deeds. The agency had to do whatever it could to block any further information that might be revealed about its deadly plans.

On June 19, 1975, the *Chicago Tribune* printed the headline REPORT CIA SCHEME TO POISON CASTRO. The short article stated, "The assassination plot . . . was directed by Sam Giancana and John Rosselli, two alleged crime syndicate figures, recruited by the CIA as middlemen for the job. Sam Giancana was installed in a suite at the Fontainebleau Hotel in Miami." In the same issue, recent presidential candidate Pat Buchanan had an editorial titled SANCTIONING ASSASSINATIONS in which he stated, "Last Sunday Vice President Nelson Rockefeller implied that the Kennedys were aware of assassination schemes being drawn up over at the CIA Headquarters." On that same day the *New York Times* headlined a story 1961 CIA POISON PLOT REPORTED AGAINST 3 TOP LEADERS IN CUBA. The article indicated, "The plot . . . was directed by Sam Giancana," and also claimed that a Senate committee was seeking a grant of immunity for Robert Maheu (also involved with Giancana) of what he knew about the Giancana-Rosselli matter. Thus these newspaper articles confirmed the CIA schemes to murder Castro as well as Sam Giancana's involvement, but they lacked further details.

Church's committee heard testimony on May 30, 1975, from an unnamed CIA chief about a financial offer to a member of the mob for a possible assassination. Only six people knew of this arrangement. On June 9 conversations were revealed between the CIA's deputy director and director of security that they needed help from the Mafia (Giancana and Rosselli) to pull off Castro's murder. Ten days later, on

June 19, no other details were known about the Castro caper. On that same day staff members of this Senate committee went to Chicago to escort Giancana back to Washington DC for his scheduled appearance before the committee on June 24, 1975.

The next scene takes place on June 19 at 1147 South Wenonah Avenue in Oak Park, Illinois, Giancana's home. The time is 9:30–9:45 p.m., and Francine, Sam's daughter, has just left the home after celebrating his return from Houston, Texas. Also leaving the house at that same time was Sam's close associate Butch Blasi. We will return to these two individuals at the end of this chapter.

At 11 p.m. on the top floor are Sam's caretaker, Joe DiPersio, and his wife. She shouts, "Joe, turn down that TV. It's so loud I can't hear myself think."

Joe shouts back, "I'm watching the *Tonight Show*. You know it's my favorite. We need the air conditioner, and it's so noisy I can't hear the TV unless it's loud. So live with it."

Meanwhile Sam Giancana has decided to fix himself one of his favorite late-night snacks—sausage and escarole—in the basement kitchen. He pauses on the ground floor and looks out the window. "Damn cars still there. Never leave me alone. What are they looking for? Why are they trying to drive me crazy? Three of them—all the time three of them. CIA, FBI, and Oak Park Police. What do they want?"

Whenever the group in one car goes on a food break, the other two groups continue the silent vigil. When the first car returns another goes. But generally there are always three.

Giancana starts to turn away then pauses. "What the hell?" He sees all three cars drive away with the CIA car leading. It is the first time this has happened. What can it mean? It's a relief but also puzzling enough to make him uneasy.

On the top floor Joe DiPersio has also seen the three cars, black as vultures, leaving together.

Sam goes down to the basement kitchen to cook his snack.

Outside, a shadowy figure has approached 1147 South Wenonah

Avenue. He stops by the side door, which many knew was always open. He quietly opens the door and steps inside, finding himself looking down into the basement area where Giancana is cooking his favorite dish. Giancana's back is to him. The figure silently descends the steps, approaches Giancana from behind, and pulls out a .22. The shot echoes in the basement room as he shoots Giancana in the back of the neck, aiming in an upward direction to the left.

Sam Giancana, Chicago mob boss and likely the most powerful don in the United States, dies quickly from this one bullet. With his foot, the assailant nudges Giancana over onto his back and puts another bullet into the front of his neck; a third entering the lower lip; a fourth, fifth, sixth, and seventh into the lower jaw and lower face. The assassin watches the blood gush out of Giancana's body then goes quietly upstairs and out of the side door, disappearing into the night.

At 11:52 Joe DiPersio says to his wife, "I'm going down to see if Mr. Giancana needs anything more from us tonight."

He halts abruptly at the sight of his boss, dead, with his face nearly shot away, rivulets of blood framing his head. "My God!" He shouts for his wife to phone the Oak Park Police at once. An ambulance arrives, picks up the body, and reaches the Oak Park Hospital emergency room at 1:40 a.m. on June 20, 1975. At 1:45 Sam Giancana is pronounced dead.

The three cars—the CIA, FBI, and Oak Park Police—return to 1147 South Wenonah and resume their silent watch.

On June 20 the major headline in the *Chicago Tribune* is MOBSTER GIANCANA MURDERED IN HIS HOME. The article stated, "Gangland Boss Sam (Momo) Giancana was found shot to death on the floor of his basement kitchen early Friday morning. In recent years Giancana's influence in the Chicago syndicate had lessened, but still was considerable. The door to the outside was open, as was the common practice." On the next day, June 21, the *Tribune*'s headline was COPS WATCHING HOME NIGHT GIANCANA SLAIN. The article indicated that the police were watching the home and "the killer who shot Giancana may have passed directly under the gaze of lawmen." Also reported was that Giancana two weeks before had met with old-time boss Tony Accardo and semiretired Cicero boss Joseph Aiuppa to confirm that he was still in good standing with the mob. The article indicated that Giancana had $1,458 in his pockets as evidence that robbery was not involved. On page 5 another headline read GIANCANA MURDER STIRS PROBLEM ON WITNESSES' SAFETY. From Lewiston, Idaho, the article quoted Frank Church, chairman of the committee investigating the CIA, "The Committee will consider protecting its witnesses after the shooting of Sam Giancana." Church added that he gave no credence to any suggestion that the CIA was in any way connected with the slaying. In Washington a source close to the CIA investigation said, "At least one on the Committee will almost certainly look into the murder of Giancana." One congressman said: "Unless there is proof that the murder was strictly a mob affair, you can bet those questions will be asked in the investigation of the CIA. Either the Senate or the House Intelligence Committee will investigate the killing." Later that year the House Committee reopened the investigation of the Kennedy murder but did not concentrate on the Giancana assassination. These articles in the press confirm many of the major points made here about Giancana's murder, including the suspicion that it may have been a CIA hit.

On the next day, June 22, a *New York Times* headline emphasized the relationship of this murder to the CIA: GIANCANA GANGSTER SLAIN, TIED TO CIA-CASTRO PLOT. The article indicated: "Neighbors reported that they saw two men in dark suits standing on the street outside Giancana's home shortly after 9 PM. Later today James Scannell, Chief of Police in Oak Park, said that two had been identified as 'law enforcement officers.' But he declined to identify them further or to explain why they were there. Police and agents of the FBI expressed surprise that Mr. Giancana had been killed with a .22 caliber weapon because crime syndicate killers usually use heavier firearms. Sen. Church acknowledged that Mr. Giancana would have been an important witness and said that the Committee was prepared to supply 'physical protection' to other witnesses." Thus on June 22, three days after Giancana's assassination, the *New York Times* strongly suggested that a CIA hit was possible.

This is a summary of the inquest on the body of Sam Giancana held before Anthony J. Bielski, deputy coroner of Cook County, Illinois, with a jury duly paneled and sworn at Polk Street, Chicago, Illinois, on July 22, 1975. A list of representatives at this inquest included Assistant State's Attorney Fredrick Crystal. The identification of Sam's remains was made by Jerome DePalma, Francine Giancana's husband. The officer present at the hearing was James Leahy (badge number 370) from the Oak Park Police. Leahy reported that at 11:53 p.m. on June 19, 1975, a call was received from 1147 South Wenonah, Oak Park, namely, the dwelling of Sam Giancana. The decedent was pronounced dead at 1:45 a.m. on June 20 at the Oak Park Hospital emergency room. The patient was dead on arrival on June 20 but really died on June 19.

The officer further testified there had been an anonymous call from 1147 Wenonah, coming through an emergency number, and the call was for an ambulance, reason unknown. When the officers arrived at the scene they found the victim, Sam Giancana, "lying on the basement floor in a pool of blood." The inquest concluded, "In my opinion the said Sam Giancana came to his death from and as a result of bullet wounds of the neck, brain, chin and mouth" and this was signed by Dr. Eupil Choi, the coroner's pathologist, and is dated June 30. There was a toxicological analysis to check for alcohol, barbiturates, tranquilizers, or narcotics. This analysis was negative and was signed by George Christopoulos, the coroner's toxicologist, and dated June 25.

The jury rendered its opinion: "From the testimony presented, we the jury find this occurrence to have been murder by person or persons unknown. We recommend that the police make a diligent search for the person or persons responsible for this act and when apprehended that he, she or they be held to the grand jury of Cook County on the charge of murder until released by due process of law."

The pathological report and protocol summarized that the victim was a white male of sixty-seven years, height of sixty-nine inches, and weight 150 pounds, with gray hair, brown iris, white sclera, and equal pupils. Another point in this pathological report was that six empty casings were recovered by the police and that there was no evidence of any forced entry. Other authors have concluded that, since there was no evidence of forced entry, Sam must have known his killer and let him into the house. Antoinette Giancana makes clear that the side door to the basement was never locked and anyone could walk in. Giancana's attitude was that no one would invade his house because he was a powerful don. Government agents knew better than to invade the home and risk prosecution, but they spent time bugging any telephone Giancana might use. Sam's killer therefore need not have been anyone he knew. Some authors, such as Bill Roemer of the FBI, mentioned a "steel door" in the basement, as if for security purposes. There was a metal door, but it was a simple storm door and came with the house when Sam purchased it.

Daughter Antoinette further describes the conditions of the night of June 19, 1975, the night that her father was killed in his house, which confirm statements made by her second husband, Robert J. "Bob" McDonnell, whom she married in 1983, six years after her father's death. "There were cars from the FBI, CIA and Oak Park Police Department that were always in front of our house, somewhat guarding but watching our home in Oak Park. On their breaks, only one car at a time would leave, return and then another car would leave. This staggering arrangement had been going on for months. Joe, the caretaker, told us he saw all three of the cars leave the family property, all at one time on the night of the murder. I believe they were ordered off the property. My father's killer would have entered the house at the basement level and that basement door was never locked. Just after the three cars left the property, my father was shot seven times, not once but seven times. They really wanted to make sure he was dead. Joe went down to see if my father was all right and discovered his body with blood all over the kitchen and made the call to the Oak Park Police Department. Then and only then did all three cars reappear. These

three cars all leaving just before my father's killing and all three returning after his death has to be more than a coincidence.

"Could his death have been prevented? Most people would believe that Sam must have had a bodyguard who had a pistol somewhere in the house. My father did not, did not, and I mean that, did
not have any bodyguards. He occasionally had someone drive him if
he had a short appointment so parking was inconvenient. But my father often did do his own driving. His group did not run around with
guns in their pockets or on their ankles. They moved around like they
were regular American citizens.

"I will tell you how I learned of Sam's assassination. My sons and I
were coming from the Wisconsin Dells, since it was a pre-birthday
present to me for my fortieth birthday. I got home that day, went to
bed, tried sleeping and tried to unwind after this road trip with the
children. All of sudden I got a call after midnight from my brother-in-
law, Jerry DePalma, and he was the one who broke the news. 'I've got
bad news for you.'

"'Oh God what happened?'

"He said that my father was dead. And then I questioned him, I
said, 'Oh, Jerry, did he die of cancer, or an infection or something like
that?' because he had just been to Houston to see Dr. Michael E. De-
Bakey.

"And he said, 'No, he was shot.'

"I did not realize that my phone was bugged, and I did say, 'If you
live by the gun, you die by the gun.' And this statement was then mentioned over the radio and TV stations. It appeared on Channel 2, CBS-
TV, with Bill Kurtis when he was a news anchor here in Chicago, since
I repeated the statement to him. I must say that Bill Kurtis did really a
thorough job of reporting my father's murder, because he was accurate
with the facts and did not add any negative comments about dad's life.

"The fact that the phone in my house had been tapped shows the
extent to which the FBI had gone. These had to have been illegal wire-
tappings, and that is extraordinary. So that shows the culture of the
time when this kind of illegal wiretapping was almost routine.

"After Sam was murdered, my life was especially difficult. First, my father and I were estranged for a couple of years, because I had discussed divorcing my first husband, Carmen Manno, which I did do eventually, and my father was strongly opposed to divorce. In July 1974 I told him that I had actually filed for divorce. He said, 'I have warned you about this and now I am disowning you.' After my father's death I was not allowed into the house at all. It seemed very strange that I couldn't even go into my father's house to look around to see what was going on. I guess there was a feeling of distrust toward me by my two sisters. Joe, my father's caretaker, was told by my sisters to call the police if I entered the property. There was a will in his possession writing me out of everything, but it was unsigned, so that made it null and void. However, we three sisters did divide whatever was there and it was only a small amount of money. I received a grand total of $56,637.64 and $6,124.60 went for inheritance taxes. Also, there was a trust with my children named in it, but my name was taken out so it made my life very rough. To this day I do not know what my father did with his enormous wealth. I would have got one-third, and my sisters would each get their third.

"We had made arrangements for my father's wake and funeral. We had a one-night wake, which was unusual since it would normally be for two nights, but my sisters decided on one night. Well, how sad it was, when there were very, very few people who attended. The two celebrities who attended were singers Phyllis McGuire and Keely Smith. The day of the funeral we had some prayers at the funeral parlor before we went to the burial place at Mount Carmel Cemetery, but there were media people out there taking pictures. Government people were taking license plate numbers, and that really bothered me. There was also a little fight at the cemetery when the press got too close to our family. Some friends of my sons grabbed the cameras away from some of the photographers.

"But there were no Mafia or Outfit people there, and absolutely nobody represented the mob here in Chicago. There weren't even any cards that expressed their condolences. I have always wondered if the absence of these people was an indicator that they were not involved in the assassination, because typically with organized crime, the people who actually did the killing are usually the first ones to show up. The killers always make a showing at the funeral, especially to send the message of their power. I have always wondered about another reason for their absence. If the government had been responsible for the murder, the mob then would not want to be involved. If it were a Mafia hit (and I absolutely do not think it was), the mob would know that their license plate numbers would be recorded by government agents and for that reason they might not have wanted to appear. One other possibility is that there was a rumor that the funeral was kind of a private family affair, so that might explain why they did not show up.

"There is another mystery. What happened to all of his properties and possessions in Mexico? He had a magnificent home, a beautiful estate. Where did all that money go? Who was in control of all of his Mexican properties that had been ransacked and looted?"

Chicago Tribune reporter Ronald Koziol reported that Sam Giancana's fortune should have totaled more than $25 million. Chuck Giancana, Sam's half-brother, in his book *Double Cross,* said that Sam was part of a ring worth billions of dollars—a joint effort based in South America, Costa Rica, and Panama. Chuck also reported that Sam's "personal take from Las Vegas . . . overall . . . was $4 million a month tax free."

Antoinette Giancana, using the Freedom of Information Act, has been stonewalled by bureaucratic roadblocks thrown up by the Drug Enforcement Department and Internal Revenue Service. Only the FBI, after nearly two years, released any documents but refused to turn over more than two thousand other pages.

Alfred P. Fredo of the Cook County Circuit Court's probate division has said that the FBI followed Giancana to Beirut more than once, but he did not have the resources to find out if Sam had financial interests in Lebanon or any other country he frequented, including the Bahamas, the Dominican Republic, England, France, Guatemala, Jamaica, Panama, Puerto Rico, and Venezuela. Fredo was also puzzled by a safe-deposit box that Sam kept in a suburban bank under the name of Sam DeTolve, which Fredo said "looked like it had been hosed out . . . that's how clean it was."

Antoinette is still searching for her father's millions or billions. One of the authors (JRH) has searched the Internet whenever a Swiss bank announces that owners of certain accounts are being sought. However we have heard that Swiss banks may absorb accounts that are not claimed after a certain number of years. This mystery, including the millions in Mexico, is unsolved.

Giancana was murdered June 19, 1975, but daughter Antoinette recalls the extreme precautions her father took throughout the years. "My father would often say, 'All of our phones are tapped, and our rooms are being tapped. Even some of the public telephones that I use are being tapped. When those damned government agents follow me, I know they can beam in on my conversation in the telephone booths. They bug any place they think I may go. You know that a government agent actually rented a room across the street from our house, and I have seen the equipment that can zero in our house. I have already got some equipment to bug them.'"

Antoinette well remembers her father taking further security measures. "He often said, 'I want the blinds and drapes closed in our house, and you won't find me walking in the dining room at night because the drapes there don't completely close.' I can picture him walking down the stairs at night all dressed in black. I'd say to him, 'Where are you going, to a funeral?' He'd say, 'No, I can walk in a crowd and nobody knows who I am. I have my collar up, my hat on with my black coat, and nobody would really recognize me.' He was even that way when I had visited him in Mexico after his retirement."

What other events led up to Sam Giancana's assassination? Some of his colleagues met untimely ends before he did. For example, his associate, Richard Cain, believed he might become the Chicago Mafia boss in 1973, and so he denounced Sam. Cain became something of a double agent, working for Giancana, on the one hand, but also for FBI agent Bill Roemer, who bugged the Giancana house and did everything possible to hound the whole family. Against Giancana's advice, Cain tried to involve himself in a business arrangement called the Cyprus Malta Gambling Venture. On December 20, 1973, Cain was murdered at the Rose Sandwich Shop in Chicago. The killer had two mismatched gloves, one was white and may have represented the white hand of the CIA, and the other was black that may well have represented the black hand of the old Sam Giancana gang of Chicago. In 2001, Michael Cain, Richard's brother, told us (JRH) the white glove represented the white-hand group his grandfather had originated. He also told us about the black glove, "You know it might be that the killer may simply have lost one glove to a matched pair."

In early July 1974 Sam was in retirement in Mexico. He was attacked in the early morning by four immigration agents at his San Cristobel estate, when he was dressed only in a robe and slippers. He was taken into custody in Mexico City, where FBI representatives assigned to the U.S. Embassy then flew him to San Antonio, Texas. In San Antonio Giancana was met by an FBI agent and given a subpoena to appear that next week at a Chicago Crime Commission grand jury. Only a minimal amount of information was given by Sam to that grand jury, and he never revealed much about his part in covert CIA operations or about the Chicago outfit, doubtless because of the well-known code of *omerta*.

This leads us to the theories about Giancana's murder. Author William Brashler in his book on Giancana speculates, "The fact that Sam was to appear before Church's committee on CIA assassinations gives rise to the belief that he had been silenced by the CIA." Church even called for a probe into the matter. Brashler further speculated, "Since [John] Rosselli and [Robert] Maheu had testified with information already damaging to the CIA, the CIA would not have had any reason to be involved in Giancana's murder." However, according to the Church Committee report, Rosselli (a Mafia don in his own right) testified five days after Giancana's murder, and Maheu testified forty days after the murder. The CIA would not have known at the time of Giancana's murder what information, if any, would be revealed by Rosselli and Maheu. Thus the agency had every reason to believe that Giancana might be the only one who could reveal its secrets. Brashler believed Giancana would have had little to add to the committee's findings, but Sam was the real leader of the plan to kill Castro and probably knew more about the plot than anyone else who might testify. Brashler further believed that it was possible the mob decided to eliminate Giancana when he returned from his retirement in Mexico, but he did not reveal any clear motivation for this possibility. Thus Brashler considered both the CIA and the mob as agents to account for Giancana's murder, and he seemed to favor the mob, but his arguments are not strong and were inconsistent with some important facts.

Charles Grimaldi was a thief who worked for Chicago mobster Sam DeStefano, and Grimaldi was a longtime informant for the Federal Bureau of Narcotics (FBN), especially to Charles Siragusa, a top officer of the FBN. Grimaldi told biographer John Kidner in 1976, "Momo [Giancana] knew too much, he was ready to talk to the Senate Investigating Committee about the Chicago underworld's part in the CIA assassination plot against Fidel Castro." A well-informed source, however, indicates that Grimaldi would not likely have credible information on this matter.

Is there evidence that the CIA killed Rosselli (a West Coast Mafia don with ties to the South American drug trade)? Around the same time in 1975, John Martino, an associate of mobster Santos Trafficante, also died. He had installed security systems in the Havana casinos owned by Trafficante and worked with Oswald's killer, Jack Ruby, when he went to Havana in 1959. Martino had been a roommate of Rosselli in Key Biscayne in Florida. Their work was to gather Cuban exiles against Castro and use mob and CIA connections to organize assassination teams. Martino's widow claimed, "The Company (i.e., CIA) or the government picked up Rosselli's body to establish the cause of death, as they determined it, claiming Rosselli had died of a heart attack." The widow was aware of how the CIA could make its own choice for anyone else's cause of death.

And more evidence exists about who planned Rosselli's murder. Bobby Baker, President Johnson's Senate secretary and "bagman," had a friend named Fred Black Jr., a major defense lobbyist in Washington. Black was a close friend and admirer of Rosselli, who stayed with Black before testifying to the Church Committee in 1975. On July 27, 1976, Black phoned Rosselli with an urgent message to get out of Miami. The next day Rosselli was murdered in Miami. These events, involving a Washington DC insider's predicting this murder, strongly suggest that Black sensed the danger to Rosselli. Martino's widow came to the same conclusion.

In 1976 James Angleton, head of counterintelligence for the CIA, blamed the Church Committee for causing the deaths of both Giancana and Rosselli by demanding their testimony on topics on which the Mafia code of silence (*omerta*) would be threatened. Angleton also admitted, in a conversation with comedian Dick Russell in June 1992, that CIA agent William Harvey was worried about what Giancana might tell the Church Committee. Angleton told Russell, "I warned Bill Harvey that Giancana would not appear." It is clear that Angleton, one of the major CIA players, would never admit that his own organization would contract Sam's death.

Another theory of Giancana's murder is that the Mafia killed him because he did not share with others in the outfit the wealth he had collected from his Latin American and Far East operations. On the other hand, Giancana lived in retirement in Mexico up to 1974 and had no direct relationship with the mob for years. Another theory is that Florida don Santos Trafficante, continuing his big business operations until 1987, was powerful enough to contract Giancana's murder if it had been ordered by the outfit. But Giancana and Trafficante had always been friends and even worked together on the Castro affair. The other powerful mobster in the United States was Carlos Marcello. But Marcello could not have been involved in the assassination since he was completely out of action, dying of Alzheimer's disease in New Orleans. Our discussion (JRH) with doctors looking after Marcello at that time revealed he was in a serious state. Another possibility is that

Trafficante was given the job by the CIA to kill Giancana. Possible evidence for this is that the .22 gun used to murder Giancana was supposedly traced to Miami, which, of course, was part of Trafficante's territory. But this evidence is clearly weak.

Could Rosselli have pulled the trigger to kill Sam? This possibility could explain Rosselli's murder to keep him quiet about the Giancana murder, since Rosselli was found in an oil drum in Florida. Other factors to explain Rosselli's murder were that he revealed some Mafia secrets in an interview with columnists Drew Pearson and Jack Anderson. Then there was his top-secret testimony before the Senate Select Committee on Intelligence. Rosselli had been deeply involved in the Mafia but also the CIA, the Bay of Pigs invasion, and the many Castro assassination attempts. He knew too much as far as the CIA was concerned. Rosselli's testimony as much as Rosselli's murder prompted the U.S. House Select Committee on Assassinations to re-open the investigation of the John F. Kennedy murder.

Information from Robert J. McDonnell, previous Cook County (Illinois) prosecutor, later Mafia lawyer and second husband to Antoinette Giancana, is crucial here for Rosselli's possible involvement in Giancana's murder. First, McDonnell's knowledge of the personality and character of John Rosselli strongly argue against Rosselli's involvement in Sam's murder. McDonnell asserted, "Rosselli could not have done this!" He confirmed for us that three automobiles were always parked in front of Giancana's house in the months prior to Giancana's murder. A few minutes before Giancana was killed, all three cars left together on a dinner break, whereas they had always staggered their breaks in the past. McDonnell's interpretation of the facts is that the CIA was responsible for the Giancana hit. Some of the strongest evidence that it was not the mob but the CIA that killed Giancana comes from a conversation McDonnell had with James "Cowboy" Mirro on the day after the murder.

Who was Cowboy Mirro? Mirro, born on December 29, 1913, was a five-foot-ten stocky man of 197 pounds. He lived in the Chicago suburb of Cicero, and his criminal record dated back to

1932, with more than ten arrests for robbery, larceny, gambling, and loan sharking. His convictions were for transporting and concealing stolen goods, which resulted in three years in the U.S. Penitentiary in Terre Haute, Indiana, and also for interstate transport of stolen money orders, which resulted in five years but was pending appeal in the late 1960s. Cowboy was his name in the mob because of his wild temperament, and he had risen to be the number-one killer for Sam Giancana. Mirro told McDonnell, "The CIA killed Sam," and McDonnell firmly believes Mirro would know if any outfit guy had been the hit man.

Antoinette Giancana believes that John F. Kennedy double-crossed her father by not giving him the protection he needed after Kennedy's election in 1960. It is her strong belief that the mob helped to kill Kennedy and the government (CIA) killed her father. The timing of the Church Committee was crucial, as was the fact that the laws regarding testimony had changed so that one could no longer take the Fifth Amendment if one were given immunity. In other words, one could either assert one's Fifth Amendment rights or have immunity, but not both. If Sam were given immunity, he would be compelled to testify. Giancana's assassination occurred after the CIA discovered that he would be accepting immunity to talk to the Church Committee.

Antoinette expands her thoughts regarding her father's death. "How would the mob profit from my father's assassination? Their only gain would be that he wouldn't talk about the alleged attempt on Castro's life. Why would they want to pop him if he only talked about Cuba? The Chicago outfit, other than Sam, really was not involved in Cuba. So what could Sam have said to the Committee to upset the Mafia? He would have nothing to say about the Chicago outfit, so I claim that the CIA came in and did this horrific thing."

FBI agent Bill Roemer, in his book *Man Against the Mob*, speculates that Butch Blasi, close assistant to Sam Giancana, could be the killer, because he had been seen going into the house close to the time of the murder. Who was Dominic "Butch" Blasi, otherwise known as Dominic De Blasa, Blasé, or Joe Bantone? He was born in 1911, was five feet six inches tall, weighed 158 pounds, and had a prominent scar on his right chin. He had been arrested thirteen times for unlawful transport of machine guns and ammunition and also for robbery. His convictions included auto theft (one year probation) and counterfeiting, with five years in the U.S. penitentiary in Terre Haute, Indiana. He served as chauffeur for Sam Giancana. Many authors claim that he was also Giancana's bodyguard, but daughter Antoinette contends, "He was not needed as a bodyguard, but was my father's constant companion and close friend." The .22 pistol, the alleged murder weapon, was found in a park preserve off of Thatcher Road, which (Roemer claimed) would have been on Blasi's way home to River Forest. But McDonnell points out that Thatcher Road would not be on Blasi's way home, and he is correct. From Giancana's Oak Park residence, the route home for Blasi was simple: north on the major street, Harlem Avenue, west on Division Street, then south on Park Avenue to 1138, his home in River Forest. Blasi would have to travel three streets farther west to get to Thatcher Road. Blasi answered no questions about the murder to the police because he knew nothing about it.

Furthermore, Roemer mentioned that Giancana's daughter Francine returned to the home that night because she had left her purse there, but Francine has continually asserted that she did not return. She left the house between 9:30 and 9:45 p.m. with Blasi. He did return at 10:15 p.m., but with his daughter, Connie Sue, who loved Sam and wanted to see him after his return from Houston. Butch and Connie Sue's visit is well known to Antoinette and Francine, and it is inconceivable that Blasi should be a suspect under these circumstances. Blasi had been Giancana's most trusted driver, and Sam considered him as a son. The possibility of his shooting Sam is out of the question, according to the Giancana family members.

Chuckie English, one of Sam's soldiers, had also been there for the welcome-home party, but he did not return after the party broke up. Giancana's third daughter, Bonnie, was not able to attend the party. She was married to Tony Tisci, administrator assistant to U.S. Congressman Roland Libonati, but later Tisci developed a severe heart condition and left politics.

Giancana's close associate Chuckie Nicoletti was murdered in 1977, immediately after the House Select Committee determined he would be called for testimony. George DeMohrenschildt, adviser to the CIA and the mob and a friend of Oswald, had also been scheduled to testify in 1977, but he died on the day he was to be questioned regarding the murder of John F. Kennedy. This death was ruled a suicide. It is noteworthy that several individuals (possibly as many as fifty) involved in the Kennedy assassination were either murdered, committed suicide, jailed, or came to some other abrupt end.

Summary

THE EVIDENCE would argue strongly against the mob's murdering Sam Giancana, especially because there was no motive for his colleagues to kill him. Also, Antoinette Giancana's husband, Bob McDonnell, believes that Cowboy Mirro would know about a mob hit if it had occurred. Both McDonnell and Mirro strongly believe that Giancana's murder was a CIA hit. The coincidence of this murder on the day staff members arrived in Chicago to accompany Giancana to Washington for testimony about the CIA's plans to murder Castro implies a motive for who likely assassinated Giancana.

6

What Really Happened

THE READER HAS DEALT with the tragic events of November 22, 1963, and the Warren Commission's interpretation of those events. We have discussed the deficiencies of that report and also have highlighted some individuals who have insight into the Kennedy assassination.

But this book cannot focus on the Kennedy assassination and exclude the murder of Sam Giancana and the link between these men. To understand Kennedy's personality and the forces that led to his demise, we need to explore the background of his father, Joseph Patrick Kennedy, a major player in his son's life. Joe's father owned a wine and spirit importation business, P. J. Kennedy and Company. The family had been dealing in the alcohol business for many years before Prohibition, when the Kennedy family made huge profits from transporting liquor from Chicago to the East Coast through the Detroit area. We will explore why the mob, called the Purple Gang, that controlled rum-running in the Detroit region had a contract on Joe Kennedy's life, because he failed to obtain their permission to run the rum. Also, New York mobster Frank Costello had another contract on Kennedy's head, because they had been business partners at one time, but Kennedy later refused to acknowledge the relationship. Joe enlisted the help of the Chicago mob to persuade the Detroit and

New York families to remove both contracts. Thus, he was twice in their debt, providing the first two links between the Kennedys and Chicago Mafia. In those early days Sam Giancana was only a minor player in the Chicago mob.

In 1919 Joseph Kennedy became manager of Hayden, Stone, and Company, where he became an expert in dealing with the stock market. In many ways he manipulated Wall Street, and when the market crashed in 1929, Joe had already made a great deal of money because he had sold off most of his holdings earlier. Some historians believe that he actually contributed to the stock market crash of 1929.

Kennedy then became involved in the movie business, using dubious tactics and methods, and latched on to a new girlfriend, actress Gloria Swanson. He made many trips with her, even though his wife and daughters were occasionally included in the party. And he continued to have significant contact with the Chicago Mafia, especially Giancana, since Sam controlled the movie business unions, representing the third link between the Kennedys and the Chicago mob.

In 1934 President Franklin Delano Roosevelt appointed Joe Kennedy to head the Security and Exchange Commission, and Kennedy outlawed those speculative and insider-trading practices that had made him rich but had also contributed to the crash of 1929. In 1937 Kennedy was appointed U.S. ambassador to Britain, but he was forced to resign in 1940 for his appeasement policies toward Adolf Hitler before World War II. Kennedy was known to be an immoral philanderer and unprincipled manipulator. After his political disgrace, Kennedy focused on the careers of his sons. Thus, the behavior of Joseph Kennedy with his philandering and the many examples of his immoral activities might well explain some of the later behavior of his son, John F. Kennedy. We will later describe how Joseph Kennedy came to Chicago to meet Sam Giancana to enlist his aid in the election of John F. Kennedy, making the huge jump from senator to president.

While John F. Kennedy was a senator, he was on various investigative committees, which were also staffed by his brother Robert. Giancana had been subpoenaed to some of these meetings and was severely embarrassed by the brothers, especially Bobby, who said Giancana "giggled like a little girl"—a fourth link.

John F. Kennedy then had aspirations to be president. And so, many promises were made by the Kennedy family to Sam Giancana, who began to work actively for the Kennedy nomination for the presidency. Giancana provided the payoffs to secure the West Virginia primary for Kennedy and thus eliminated Hubert Humphrey as a viable contender for the Democratic nomination. With Giancana's power in Chicago he was able to deliver the vote of the state of Illinois that put Kennedy over the top in the 1960 election. Chapter 7 will introduce Giancana's associate, Murray Humphreys, and the way he made certain that the union vote was solid for Kennedy in this election. It therefore seems likely that Kennedy would not have been elected to the White House without the help of Sam Giancana and the Chicago mob—a fifth link between these two powerful men. Another link, the sixth, was the removal of documents of the annulled wedding between John F. Kennedy and his first wife in 1947 with the help of the Chicago mob.

A seventh major contact between Giancana and the Kennedys was through the CIA, which pegged Sam to coordinate the assassination of Fidel Castro. This plan was clearly supported by John F. Kennedy and Attorney General Robert F. Kennedy. The CIA not only enlisted Sam Giancana but also Johnny Rosselli and Santos Trafficante, who controlled Mafia operations in the state of Florida. Although Giancana and his associates were unsuccessful in assassinating Castro, they viewed themselves as working for the government, and the government, of course, was headed by the Kennedy brothers. About six months after the election, Sam Giancana had every reason to believe his efforts to help Kennedy in the election were going to pay off; he had been promised so much from the Kennedy family. There are many examples of the apparent cooperation between Kennedy and Giancana in memos from the president to Sam and an open door to the Oval Office for Giancana's associates.

Quite suddenly, however, Kennedy's attitude toward the Mafia changed. There were no more memos to Giancana. Promises to allow the return of some exiled mob figures were broken. And visits to the White House were no longer allowed. Around that same time, the FBI instituted continuous and constant surveillance in a lock-step monitoring of every activity of Sam Giancana (an eighth link). The FBI was, of course, under the attorney general, Robert F. Kennedy, and, therefore, it was the Kennedys who were contributing to this misery in the life of Giancana. Father Joseph had maintained that there was still a positive relationship between his family and Giancana and that the FBI's efforts were just to "make it look good." In summary, it seems likely that John F. Kennedy would not have been elected president of the United States without the help of Giancana and his mobsters. The promises were that the mob would have an easy time under the Kennedy administration, but instead, the Kennedys double-crossed Giancana and made his life miserable through continuous monitoring of his every move by the FBI.

Another major disappointment for Sam Giancana was that he had established a shrimp business in Cuba and had put millions of dollars into that industry. After Fidel Castro came to power, this business was taken away from him. But the Kennedy administration had plans to depose Castro, and Sam's shrimp business would be restored. However, the Bay of Pigs invasion to oust Castro turned out to be a disaster for the Cuban refugee army out to reclaim their country. We will make clear that it was a political decision (to avoid appearing as an aggressor to the UN) and not a military one that persuaded Kennedy to hold up the second group of bombers from Nicaragua that were to provide air support for the invading force. Therefore, because of a political decision, Kennedy allowed the Bay of Pigs effort to fail and more than one hundred soldiers were killed and more than a thousand were tortured and imprisoned. Because of Kennedy's failure at the Bay of Pigs, the possibility of restoring a lucrative shrimp industry to Giancana ended—a ninth link.

Another relationship between Kennedy and Giancana as a tenth link was through Judith Campbell, a beautiful woman whom Frank

Sinatra had introduced to Kennedy. Campbell became one of Kennedy's mistresses, and she was also a mistress of Sam Giancana. In the 1960 election, Judith played a major role. On some occasions Giancana had discussions with the president in her hotel room. Then Kennedy stopped seeing her, refused to take her phone calls at the White House, and J. Edgar Hoover became involved. Although this link between Kennedy and Giancana seemed to cease at that time, Campbell spent more time with Giancana, who enjoyed a physical relationship with her. Perhaps the crowning blow contributing to the rage of Giancana against the Kennedys was when Campbell became pregnant, allegedly by John F. Kennedy. Giancana had to make arrangements for her abortion in Chicago. This abortion was an important eleventh link. Sam, whose wife had died, even offered to marry Campbell. Judith refused.

The links between John F. Kennedy and Sam Giancana through the CIA became increasingly important, and this agency turned out later to be a common enemy for both men. The CIA had developed the plans for the Bay of Pigs invasion, and when it ended in disaster, Kennedy blamed the CIA, claiming that he "would break it into a thousand pieces." He then proceeded to fire all the major players in the CIA. There were many in the agency who were very upset over Kennedy's action, because they believed it was his fault that the invasion had failed and yet he blamed the CIA. Some evidence points to an involvement of rogue elements of the CIA in Kennedy's assassination, likely as a reaction to this breakup. And chapter 8 presents the evidence that the CIA killed Giancana. Link number twelve is that the CIA was probably involved in the assassination of both men.

FBI Director J. Edgar Hoover and President Kennedy were political enemies, and there was a deep hatred between the two. Hoover had held the director's position for many decades, and his major focus was to continue in that capacity beyond the accepted age for federal retirement. The Kennedys, however, were determined to remove him. Furthermore, Attorney General Robert F. Kennedy was Hoover's administrative boss and severely embarrassed and insulted him on many occasions. The president's affairs with many women was well known to Hoover, who presented himself as a man of high ethical and moral standards and pretended to be outraged by these exploits of the president. Hoover knew that an assassination was going to take place, but he did nothing about it and therefore can be considered as an accomplice or a conspirator. A later chapter will explain why Hoover is our choice as the likely coordinator of the different groups that wanted Kennedy removed from power. Thus, there was a link, number thirteen, between Giancana and Kennedy through the association of not only the CIA but also the FBI. A decade after Kennedy's death, the FBI kidnapped Giancana from his Mexican estate in 1974, placed him on an airplane to San Antonio, and sent him to testify before the Chicago Crime Commission. Therefore, certain elements of the CIA and the FBI turned against Kennedy and Giancana and likely contributed to the assassination of both men.

Four other mob figures figured significantly in the assassination of John F. Kennedy. The one most likely involved was Carlos Marcello. He was the don of the New Orleans area, although his empire spread throughout the South, including Dallas. Marcello was an illegal resident, and Robert F. Kennedy chose to use this fact to remove Marcello from the country. We will describe how Robert F. Kennedy illegally kidnapped Marcello and his lawyer in New Orleans, flew them to Central America, had them driven into the jungles of El Salvador and Guatemala, and left them there possibly to die. Marcello nearly did die in his attempt to return to civilization; he broke three ribs and was in considerable pain in his escape from the jungle. Eventually, he did return to the United States and sued Robert F. Kennedy for this kidnapping. He was never lawfully deported.

As in the case with other mob figures, Marcello had been harassed by the Kennedys and had developed a deep hatred toward them. After many attempts by Attorney General Kennedy to deport Marcello, there was a final decision of the courts that Marcello would remain in the country. The headlines in the *New Orleans Times-Picayune* for this victory were in larger letters than for the assassination of President

Kennedy, which had occurred on the same day. One can understand the motivation behind Carlos Marcello in trying to be rid of Kennedy and will note the evidence by statements made by one of his associates that Marcello directly contributed to the assassination of the president.

Santos Trafficante of Florida was another major mob figure. Trafficante owned many hotels in Cuba, and when Castro took over that island, Trafficante lost millions of dollars from the casinos and hotels that were seized. Not only was he harassed in the same way that the other Mafia dons were hounded by the FBI, but he had counted on the Bay of Pigs invasion to restore his hotel and casino empire in Havana. Trafficante was aware that Kennedy made a political decision when he decided against allowing the bombers to take off from Nicaragua to provide air support for the troops at the Bay of Pigs. This decision resulted in Cuba's remaining in Castro's hands. Thus, Kennedy, for his own political ends, was responsible for the continued loss of Trafficante's income of millions of dollars from his Cuban empire. We will introduce Frank Ragano, the attorney for Santos Trafficante, and how he reported the confession made by this mobster of his involvement in the Kennedy assassination.

The fourth individual involved in this assassination was Jimmy Hoffa, head of the Teamster's Union in Detroit. Perhaps no one believed he had suffered more under the harassment of Robert F. Kennedy. The attorney general was unrelenting in his efforts to destroy Hoffa and the Teamster's Union. The role played by Hoffa in getting rid of John F. Kennedy will become clear, as will the role of Frank Ragano in delivering an important message from Hoffa to other Mafia figures.

John F. Kennedy had developed serious enemies among other groups. The anti-Castro Cubans who had trained for the invasion at the Bay of Pigs were incensed at Kennedy's political decision to refuse to allow the bombers to make certain success of this mission. The CIA recoiled at Kennedy's blaming the agency for the failure at the Bay of Pigs and his vow to break it into a thousand pieces. There were other reasons why many in the CIA became enemies of the president. One

National Security Action Memo (NSAM) essentially downgraded the CIA, restricted its area of influence to intelligence gathering, and gave more power to the Joint Chiefs of Staff. The CIA became a group to collect data rather than to take action.

Another Kennedy order, NSAM No. 263, very much upset another segment of the community. This memo was issued during the Vietnam War and indicated that Kennedy planned to withdraw troops quickly and eventually remove all U.S. troops from this territory. The military-industrial complex, which was providing the war machine for this conflict, immediately saw that its profits would be grossly curtailed if this withdrawal were carried out. There were many organizations that contributed to this war machine, and all of them could see what effect the NSAM would have on their profits. One major scandal that created other enemies for Kennedy was the awarding of a $6.5 billion contract for the TFX fighter (F111) solely on the basis of a political gain for a reelection in 1964 rather than on objective grounds.

Finally, one other organization contributed toward the assassination of John F. Kennedy: the FBI. As mentioned earlier, there was intense hatred between the Kennedys and Hoover. Vice President Johnson, on the other hand, was very friendly with Hoover. This insight is compounded by shocking statements allegedly made by Johnson to his mistress that indicate he had foreknowledge of Kennedy's assassination.

After having established the motivation behind the Mafia and other organizations to get rid of John F. Kennedy, this conspiracy theory must show that Lee Harvey Oswald was not responsible for the assassination of the president. The first major point regarding Oswald is to show that he had close ties to the mob and perhaps even the Dallas Police Department. Note that his uncle, early serving as a stepfather, was a member of the Marcello crime organization in New Orleans, and that an associate of Marcello bailed Oswald out of jail at one time. Another associate of Marcello was David Ferrie who had had contact with Oswald in the Civil Air Patrol and traveled with him to various parts of Louisiana. We will point out the relationships with nightclub owner Jack Ruby, who murdered Oswald, and how they had been seen together, most often in Ruby's nightclub, the Carousel. There were clear associations between Oswald and private investigator Guy Banister, who had worked for both the FBI and CIA. Oswald used Banister's address on pamphlets that he handed out on New Orleans streets. Even Oswald's mother indicated the close relationship that her son had with the FBI and CIA. Oswald also had a friendship with oil engineer George DeMohrenschildt, who had worked for the FBI and CIA and also had close ties to the Mafia. Finally, convincing evidence came to light soon after the assassination that there was a relationship between Oswald and the Dallas Police Department.

Arguments against Oswald as the lone assassin can be viewed as positive evidence for a planned, coordinated conspiracy to murder the president. One comes from Silvia Odio, whose father led an anti-Castro effort. She met a man named Leon Oswald. According to Odio, Leon said that Kennedy would be assassinated in the near future. Also, entertainer and dancer Rose Cheramie had stated two days before the assassination that the murder of Kennedy was to take place soon. Finally, right-winger Joseph Milteer can be heard on videotape two weeks before the assassination asserting that Kennedy was to be killed.

There are many facts in evidence that argue strongly against Oswald as the lone gunman who killed Kennedy. First, he was a poor shot with a very cheap, misaligned rifle; the six to ten shots that likely were fired in seven to eight seconds could not have come from this inferior weapon. The facts about where Oswald was in the Texas School Book Depository, just before the shots rang out, argue strongly against his direct involvement in the assassination. His unhurried exit from the depository and inconclusive paraffin tests on his hands and face represent further evidence. As previously mentioned, considerable evidence exists that Oswald was associated with the Mafia, CIA, and FBI, and therefore was not in anyway a lone conspirator.

We have established the strong motivation on the part of three major Mafia figures (as well as Jimmy Hoffa) to eliminate John F. Kennedy. The Giancana, Trafficante, and Marcello groups each sent two shooters who were likely placed in the Dal-Tex and Texas School Book Depository buildings. The evidence is overwhelming that the bullet that actually killed Kennedy and nearly removed the right hemisphere of his brain came from the grassy knoll. The individual who fired that shot was part of the Giancana team (a fourteenth link), and we have chosen to call him "Deadeye." He is presently in prison for life in Illinois, blamed for shooting a policeman. Investigative reporter Joe West had become aware of Deadeye from a retired FBI agent and, after considerable persuasion, managed to interview him. Deadeye finally permitted a videotaped interview, now in the authors' possession. He had previously been a stock-car driver and was part of the Eighty-second Airborne Division. Later he became involved in the CIA and the training of anti-Castro Cubans for the Bay of Pigs invasion. His early life led him to become an assistant to Chuckie Nicoletti, an important hit man in Sam Giancana's Chicago mob. In the video interview, Deadeye discusses his trip from Chicago to Dallas as part of the Giancana team to eliminate Kennedy. You will read all the details of what was done in preparation for the assassination. Nicoletti then detailed Deadeye as the shooter at the grassy knoll, using the "Fireball" weapon, a handgun with a telescopic sight that used exploding, fragmenting bullets.

One of the major points in this book is that a review of the recently released, cleaned-up film of Kennedy's assassination, taken by Abraham Zapruder, clearly shows the slamming of Kennedy's body to his left side after he was shot on the right side of his head. This violent movement could only be the result of the force of a bullet coming from his right side, the grassy knoll, and cannot be explained by any type of reflex. The CIA and FBI had understandable reasons to discredit this shooter and to characterize him as a fraud. After all, his presence on the grassy knoll and his success in shooting the bullet that killed Kennedy would essentially mean that these two organizations had failed to protect the president. A letter from Sam Giancana's daughter, Antoinette, would likely settle the matter as to whether or not Deadeye is a phony. If he had made up this story and wanted only attention, he would have no reason to respond to Antoinette's letter, which would likely expose him as a phony. If, on the other hand, Deadeye is genuine about his role in this assassination, he might well respond and did so in a warm and cordial letter to Antoinette. Later, Antoinette and her husband traveled to the prison, interviewed him, and found he was convincing about his role in the assassination. As further evidence in favor of Deadeye's credibility, a later interview by Antoinette with a motel owner with mob ties verified this shooter's close relationship with Chuckie Nicoletti and the Chicago mob. The authors of this book firmly believe that Deadeye fired the head shot from the grassy knoll that killed President Kennedy.

A devil's advocate position is taken in questioning all aspects of Deadeye's claims. The first asks why relatively few individuals know about the taped interview that the authors presently possess. The answer will be clear in chapter 15. The next question is whether Deadeye only wanted to draw attention to himself, that he was not really involved in the assassination. We will relate what is on the tape and how convincing he was about his motivation.

His background in the military could be questioned as to whether he really was part of the Eighty-second Airborne, but evidence comes from an individual who was a member of the Eighty-second Airborne that the grassy knoll gunman had indeed been part of this unit. One could argue that there could not be confirmation of the military records on Deadeye, but this problem is easily explained. Our gunman tells the story that Johnny Rosselli had made his way to Dallas on a military air transport service flight from Washington DC. Another pilot, however, claimed that he had flown Rosselli there from New Orleans. Deadeye could only report what Rosselli had told him and did so. The way Rosselli got to Dallas has not been totally settled, but it is not a significant fact in this story. One could raise the question as to why Deadeye was told only two hours before the assassination that he would be one of the shooters. Reasonable answers are given to this question. Deadeye makes clear the details of the Fireball gun and speaks at length about the shots with the mercury load associated with frangible bullets. When one views the assassination through the Zapruder film, an exploding bullet into the right hemisphere of Kennedy's brain becomes clear. Our gunman's weapon and its frangible shot explain what is very evident on the film.

Deadeye claimed that he took the shell from the bullet that killed Kennedy and bit down on it so his teeth marks were on the casing, leaving it on the grassy knoll. An individual found this casing in 1987. Furthermore, a dentist has confirmed that the marks on this shell were teeth marks from a human. This statement from the dentist was made many months after our gunman had made his claim. Finally, Deadeye indicated that he saw various Mafia and CIA individuals at the assassination site, and others have confirmed that these individuals were present.

The major point here is that even casual observation of the body of John F. Kennedy when the bullet hit his right hemisphere shows his body slammed to the left side, indicating clearly that a shot had to come from the right side, the grassy knoll. The authors firmly believe that this shot was fired by Deadeye.

The November 1963 assassination is now set in the context of the Church Committee in 1975 that investigated CIA plans to assassinate five heads of state. The targeted individuals were Chile's Rene Schneider, the Congo's Patrice Lumumba, Cuba's Fidel Castro, the Dominican Republic's Rafael Trujillo, and South Vietnam's Ngo Dinh Diem. Four of these assassinations were successful. Castro escaped the assassination attempt that was headed up by Sam Giancana, Santos Trafficante, and Johnny Rosselli, all of whom were hired by the CIA. Audiotapes from the John F. Kennedy Library made public in 1988 indicate that the president admitted some responsibility in one of the assassination attempts. A CIA operation, called Mongoose, was designed to explore the killing of Castro. This scheme began in November 1961, lasted at least for a year, and was likely coordinated by Robert F. Kennedy.

Testimony before the Church Committee was heard on May 30, 1975, when an unnamed support chief of the CIA discussed only the

financial arrangements of the intended killers of Castro. The next testimony was on June 9, 1975, and was from the CIA Deputy Director
Richard Bissell, who spoke briefly of the plans to use the mob and indicated that he only briefly mentioned these plans to his own administration. One of the major points in this book is the incredible
coincidence between the timing of members from the Church Committee coming from Washington DC to Chicago to escort Giancana to
give testimony to the Church Committee and Giancana's assassination
on June 19, 1975. He was killed just before he was scheduled to appear before this committee, and at that time very few details had been
given about the plans to kill Castro. Johnny Rosselli of the mob gave
testimony five days after Giancana was killed and later was also murdered. William Harvey of the CIA testified on June 25 with a few more
details added by Robert Maheu, the man who was the link between
the mob and the CIA. His testimony was on July 29, 1975. Thus, it
will be clear that at the time of Giancana's murder only a few details of
the CIA plans to murder Castro had been given to the Church Committee, and a reasonable assumption is that the CIA did not want Giancana to testify. As an example of the tactics of the CIA around the
time of the assassination of Giancana, this agency, embarrassed by the
Senate Committee, threatened Senator Frank Church to make certain
that he would not be a candidate for either president or vice president
of the United States.

The one point that has been often mentioned in reports about Giancana's assassination is the assumption that he obviously knew his
killer since there was no sign of a break-in at the house. A major
point, revealed by his daughter Antoinette, is that this assumption is
completely false. The point that he knew his killer because he must
have let him into the home is absolutely invalid.

Could the mob have murdered Sam Giancana? The description of
Sam's life during the few years before his murder will diminish any
concern that the mob killed him. A conversation between Antoinette's
husband, Robert McDonnell, and Sam's lawyer and Giancana's major
hit man, Cowboy Mirro, provides powerful evidence that it was not

the mob but the CIA that killed Giancana. The so-called coincidence of Giancana's murder just before he was to testify to the Church Committee, and the fact that the CIA would have been embarrassed by his testimony, would argue strongly that the agency was involved in his assassination. Thus certain groups of the CIA had become an enemy of both President John F. Kennedy and Chicago don Sam Giancana.

Many links exist between the Kennedys, mainly John F. Kennedy, and the Chicago Mafia, mainly Sam Giancana. They include the removal of two contracts on father Joseph Kennedy by the Chicago mob, the interaction between Joe Kennedy and Sam Giancana in Hollywood, the interaction between John F. Kennedy and Robert F. Kennedy with Sam Giancana during Senate investigation committees, the significant aid given to John F. Kennedy for his election as president, removal of documents of John F. Kennedy's first marriage, and the interaction of the two men in the attempt to kill Castro. Other links are the continuous monitoring of Giancana's moves, especially by Robert F. Kennedy, the loss of Sam's shrimp business because of John F. Kennedy's failure in the Bay of Pigs, sharing of girlfriend Judith Campbell, her abortion, probable involvement of the CIA and FBI in the assassinations of both Kennedy and Giancana, and finally, the involvement of one of Giancana's men, Deadeye, as the killer of President Kennedy.

7

The Double Cross

Sᴀᴍ Gɪᴀɴᴄᴀɴᴀ, ᴛʜᴇ sᴏɴ of Antonio and Antonia Giancana, was born on June 15, 1908, in Chicago, although he celebrated his birthday on July 15. He was named Momino Salvatore Giancana and often called Mo. Sam's very young mother gave birth to two children, a boy and a girl. Soon after the second child was born, his mother died, probably from cancer, and his father married for a second time. This new wife gave birth to six other children. Sam was slowly but surely moved out of the house, and he developed feelings of rage. As he grew older, he told his daughter Antoinette, he developed a great amount of anger because he was not getting the attention he should have received from either his father or his stepmother. When his stepmother died, his father married a third wife, a cousin to the second wife, who brought to the marriage even more children.

Sam's father was a strict disciplinarian, and this brought out a rebellious streak in Sam. In the book *Double Cross* by Sam's half brother Chuck, on one occasion Sam's father chained him to a tree. His sister told Antoinette that it did not happen, but his half brothers claim that it did. Sam's father would also lock him up in the attic for disciplinary reasons. The family was also having a hard time financially. Sam's father was in the produce and grocery business and selling illegal liquor on the side. Antoinette remembers her father saying that, when he was younger, he resented the way they lived from hand to mouth. He did not want his life to turn out that way. He wanted to progress and do something a little better than his father. Antoinette remembers him saying "When I was a kid, I decided I was going to try to help my family and make things a little easier and nicer." Still, he was very angry and distraught over his family and tired of living barely above poverty. Early on this attitude triggered his involvement with the wrong crowd. As a young kid on the streets of Chicago, in the Lexington and California area (West Side), he stole cookies from his own father's grocery store. His father caught him periodically, lectured him, and spanked him. To his way of thinking, however, Sam was not stealing; he was taking what he thought was rightfully his—his cookies out of the jar in his father's store.

Even at a young age Sam had a great sense of organization. He developed the 42 Gang, teenage hoodlums who roamed the streets and terrorized the neighborhood. He was very successful at that. Temperamentally, in those early years, his mood suddenly shifted from Dr. Jekyll to Mr. Hyde, and that continued throughout his life. At one moment he could be the most generous man on earth, bringing home little tokens of remembrance to his children when he'd return from trips full of affection. But there was a horrific second side, when he'd become violent, yelling and screaming. As Antoinette grew older, and especially now, she understood her father's anger and hostility but also his love.

Another example of opposites in Sam's character was his attitude toward people. His attitude toward men was very different from his attitude toward women. From the time he was a young man he thought that women had their place in society: they should stay home, raise the family, tend to the house, and not be seen in public. Before his daughters could leave the house, they had to have proper clothing as well as proper manners. And they could not talk to strangers, nor could his wife.

There was not only a romantic but also an exceptional, sensitive, artistic side of Giancana. First, he collected figurines and ivory and other art objects imported from France, Germany, Italy, and just about everywhere in the world. He became a gemologist on his own; he knew gems, carried them when he traveled, and would carry a little eyepiece to examine them. He knew precisely what an emerald should look like, the characteristics of rubies and other stones, imperfections in them, their color, clarity, and all other aspects. He had a great knowledge of pearls, but he had an interest in gems for another reason. They were a thing of beauty to him, but they also represented an insurance policy should the economy go bad suddenly. He would have gold, diamonds, emeralds, rubies, pearls, and other major gems in case of emergency. Most of the stones he collected were not set in platinum or gold; they were always loose in envelopes. Each of the many packages of diamonds had a carat weight on them as well as the clarity indicated. These gems would be his means of escape or his means of supporting his family.

Sam's technical intelligence, not only about gambling machines, but also of how deals worked and how people should be organized, was way beyond the other members of his Mafia. He could well have been chief executive officer of some large multinational corporation. Sam's sense of organization appeared even in his personal life. Antoinette remembers the way he meticulously kept his clothes in his closet. Everything had to be folded to perfection. He organized the whole household, everything was in its place and was very neat. She remembers Sam had a little telephone book he carried with him that was in code. He would take down phone numbers and code them in a way that only he could understand. No one could decode his address book.

Meanwhile, Sam developed his professional skills and was known as a very good "wheelman," an expert driver of cars, even at a young age. By 1923, because of his wild behavior, he was considered a moony type and was often called Mooney instead of Mo, his previous nickname. At fifteen years of age he worked for Diamond Joe Esposito who had put together a very powerful gang in the Chicago area. In

1924 Esposito was one of the most powerful men in Chicago and, some believed, a major figure in all of North America. In addition to Esposito, Sam had gained favor with the Al Capone gang. By June 1928, when he was twenty years old, nearly all those in the Italian community feared but also revered him. When Giancana was twenty-nine years old, Chicago Mafia chiefs Paul Ricca and Murray Humphreys were very much impressed with him. Sam liked their renegade style as he watched these two bosses get what they wanted by fixing politicians, using clever schemes, and wiping out their enemies whenever they felt it was necessary.

At that time, bootlegger Joseph P. Kennedy had survived a near-fatal scrape with the Detroit Jewish Mafia, the Purple Gang. They had a contract on Joe for bringing his rum through their territory without permission. According to the Giancana family, Joe Kennedy came to Chicago and begged Esposito to do something about this contract. A call was made by Esposito to get rid of the contract, and it was done. So Kennedy was now in debt to the Chicago mob. This debt is the first link between the Chicago Mafia and the Kennedys.

In 1942 Mafia chief Paul Ricca was sent to prison for ten years, appointing Tony Accardo as the boss of the Chicago underworld in his place. Giancana continued to move up in the Mafia organization, and in 1946 he was considered an underboss to Accardo. In December 1946 Lucky Luciano of the New York mob called for a meeting of the so-called Commission in Havana, and at that time Giancana was considered completely accepted into the Mafia. This was also his introduction to Cuba. In her book *Mafia Princess,* Antoinette Giancana makes clear that her father had a great interest in Havana's casino and shrimp industries, and before Castro's takeover Sam traveled to Miami and Cuba as often as once a week.

In 1947 Meyer Lansky, financial genius of the mob, was appointed by Luciano as the regent in Cuba, especially because Lansky had a close relationship with dictator Fulgencio Batista. Lansky had persuaded Batista to quit in 1944 but later helped him return to the Cuban Senate and still later as dictator in 1952. Lansky developed the concept of hotel-casino groups in Cuba, like those in Las Vegas today, and many of the Mafia wanted to be part of the action in Havana. For example, Santos Trafficante of the Florida mob tried to make a deal directly with Batista but instead was referred to Lansky, who controlled the casino business in Cuba. Lansky later helped Sam, who had his own genius in understanding a gambling empire. An important meeting took place between them at the Acapulco Towers in Mexico. Lansky complimented Sam by saying, "You're the only Italian who handles money like they do in the Jewish mob."

Giancana was traveling to many areas, including Florida, Central America, Las Vegas, but especially to Cuba to inspect his business. Daughter Antoinette remembers well that every time the family went to Florida, Sam went off to Cuba, almost on a weekly basis. She remembers that he said, "Dictator Batista is in my pocket. I enjoyed working with him."

In 1948 millions of dollars were poured into the Cuba casinos by Luke Mooney and his syndicate, but by the middle of 1955, both Tony Accardo and Paul Ricca of the Chicago mob were being investigated by the IRS. These investigations threatened their positions in the syndicate. At a private party at the Tam O'Shanter Country Club in Niles, a northern suburb of Chicago, Sam Giancana was formally made the boss of the Chicago outfit. Antoinette points out, "My father spent his entire adult life in the Mafia, so it was appropriate he was made the boss. However, he had nothing to do directly with Al Capone himself." She relates a story that is confirmed by a few people whom she has known well personally. Her father kidnapped Tony Accardo and held him for several hours, maybe a couple of days. This event showed that Sam had potential to do extraordinary things, and to kidnap Accardo was very out of the ordinary. That kidnapping episode may be why Sam was esteemed to be a better leader than Accardo; Sam was smarter. He could outsmart anybody else in the Mafia, and his intelligence in business deals may have created a consensus that Sam would be better than Accardo at running the program. After Sam's rise to fame, however, Accardo remained CEO (chief executive officer) as an active adviser and never gave up that position. Antoinette says, "Even after his so-called retirement, one could tell that Accardo had something special, and other members of the outfit had great respect for him."

In 1956 Giancana was "the Man" in Chicago. Joe Kennedy certainly recognized that power and counted on it when he made arrangements to contact Sam Giancana in May 1956. According to the Giancana family, Kennedy wanted Giancana to come to the East Coast, but Sam insisted on a meeting in Chicago. Three days later Kennedy met with Sam in a suite at Chicago's Ambassador East Hotel. The reason for this meeting was to remove another contract on Joe Kennedy. This new problem was Joe's business associate, Frank Costello of the New York mob. In New York, Costello had a major falling out with Joe Kennedy because Joe did not want to take care of the financial obligations he had made with his former New York pals. Costello had been partners with Joe during Prohibition and had even delivered some bootleg scotch to a Cape Cod beach party, celebrating the tenth reunion of Joe's Harvard Class of 1912 (according to author Seymour Hersh). Furthermore, Costello believed the mob had helped make Kennedy rich, and now he was calling in a marker. Joe felt that he would be embarrassed to be associated with the old New York group now that his son was moving ahead in politics. Costello apparently had a contract out on Joe Kennedy because Joe thought he was just too high and mighty to associate with Frank. This Costello contract represents the second link between the Kennedys and the Chicago Mafia.

The business world was again the center for another relationship between the Kennedys and the Chicago mob. Father Joe Kennedy had made a financial killing in Hollywood in the 1920s and 1930s with the help of some union muscle provided by the New York and Chicago mobs. In 1934 the Chicago group backed fellow bootlegger Joe Kennedy and allowed him a successful entry into the motion-picture industry. The mob took its union control to a national level by placing a local man, George Browne, as president of the International Alliance of

Theatrical Stage Employees and Motion Picture Operators. Browne was allegedly controlled by Willie Bioff, who was part of Al Capone's gang. This move gave the Chicago group control over Hollywood's film industry and the theaters where the films were shown. This move is a third link between the Chicago Mafia and the Kennedys.

In the 1950s Joe Kennedy, concerned about the Kennedy image, tried to distance himself from his old cronies, not only those in New York, but throughout the mob. In Chicago the consensus was, "If there ever was a crook, it was Joe Kennedy." Still earlier, in 1947, he had called upon Sam Giancana to take care of a nasty problem. John F. Kennedy, a Catholic, had married Durie Malcolm, an Episcopalian and a Palm Beach socialite. Her maiden name was Kerr, but she took the name of her stepfather. She had divorced her first husband, Firmin Des Ioge IV, and was divorced by her second husband, F. John Barsback, on January 24, 1947. Joe Kennedy told Sam Giancana, "I need to have this marriage annulled without publicity and with absolutely no record of it—no trace of any legal documents." Sam directed mobster Johnny Rosselli to handle that matter, a sixth link between the Kennedys and the Chicago mob. Seymour Hersh, in his 1997 account, indicated that it was not the mob but Charles Spalding, a friend of Kennedy and local attorney in Palm Beach, Florida, who removed all the wedding documents related to the marriage by a justice of the peace in an early morning ceremony. There was no evidence of a divorce here, and the well-known Cardinal Cushing of Boston once referred to the matter, claiming that marriage outside of the Catholic Church would not require an annulment, but only a "nullifying declaration."

When Fidel Castro came to power on New Year's Eve in 1959, Sam Giancana had to take the first plane home. Sam always spoke of the millions of dollars he lost in Cuba. Antoinette remembers that her father was disheartened that no sooner was everything organized in Cuba, buying the shrimp boats and so forth, then Castro came in and took over. Antoinette believed Castro was a dynamic person and was somewhat impressed with him. Sam was upset with her impression of

Castro and actually became violent and very angry when she even mentioned his name. Castro was a thorn in her father's side. Sam was never able to forgive Castro for taking away his investment in Cuba. Antoinette, however, knows that her father once said he had no intentions of killing Castro, none at all, and he just chuckled when he said to her, "Just think we're making lots of money off of the U.S. government; it's about time we take from them, instead of them taking from us." He was very firm on that. She would call this a double double cross of the Kennedys. In other words, Sam double crossed the Kennedys by failing to assassinate Castro, and then, because of that failure, the Kennedys were angry with Sam and therefore double crossed him by not giving him the cooperation he expected during the Kennedy administration.

In January 30, 1957, Robert F. Kennedy was on the Senate's McClellan Committee to investigate organized crime, but in Chicago the word came to the Mafia from father Joe Kennedy that "everything was under control." Six months later, Sam Giancana said, "I am going to follow this Senate Investigation Committee closely because Robert F. Kennedy has planned a full-scale attack on our world." Giancana questioned, "What was wrong with that Kennedy brat," but Joe continued to reassure Sam that he had everything under control, another example of a link between the two families. Sam saw Robert F. Kennedy as a calculating, ruthless, ambitious man (much like himself), and on November 27, 1957, J. Edgar Hoover launched his Top Hoodlum Program (THP) against organized crime. In Chicago at least ten agents were assigned to this program, mostly to tail Sam.

In early 1959 Sam Giancana made a major decision and said, "I am going to support John F. Kennedy for president." This was the important fifth link between Sam Giancana and John F. Kennedy. Just before Christmas 1959, Sam announced, "If I could help get Jack elected, then I could get Bobby off the McClellan Committee."

One other reason Giancana supported Kennedy and not Richard M. Nixon for president is explained by his daughter Antoinette. "Nixon's best friend was Charles Gregory Rebozo, called Bebe, who was born

November 17, 1912, in Tampa, Florida, of Cuban parents. Although he married Claire Green at age eighteen years, this marriage was annulled three years later, but he remarried her in 1946, then later married another woman, named Jane Lucke. Bebe was a self-made millionaire, a real estate developer, and banker. I had met him in Ciro's nightclub in Miami while he was having dinner with Nixon. I had two dates with him in 1957. Although I have not revealed this before, he date-raped me both times in the Conrad Hilton Hotel in Chicago, not knowing my identity until after the second date. When I returned to my father's house, he saw my condition, and I think he knew what Nixon's best friend had done to me. This may be one powerful reason that my father favored Kennedy over Nixon."

Meanwhile, Joe Kennedy had decided to dance with the devil. He believed he could play with fire and not get burned, because he had survived two contracts from the Mafia. Father Joe felt that he was safe and that his son was also safe from any revenge.

During the 1960 campaign John F. Kennedy worried that he might not win some of the primaries before the November election. An arrangement was made that Sam Giancana would take care of the very important West Virginia primary, but only if certain promises were made by Kennedy. One promise was that, after the election, Joe Adonis of the mob would be allowed to return to the United States; he had been deported in 1953. The two families agreed. There were many votes to be bought in West Virginia, so Giancana sent mobster Skinny D'Amato, a New Jersey nightclub owner, with a suitcase of money to buy votes so that Kennedy would win the West Virginia primary rather than the popular candidate, Hubert Humphrey. The Chicago outfit put half a million dollars, mostly Sam's money, into that primary, and as a result, Kennedy defeated Humphrey by 29 percent. Little else stood in the way of the nomination for Kennedy after that.

Lyndon B. Johnson was put on the ticket as vice president after he and the powerful Speaker of the House of Representatives, Sam Rayburn, had a "talk" with Kennedy. Murray Humphreys's control over sixty-one unions also helped to secure the victory for John F.

Kennedy. On November 8, 1960, there were many calls from Frank Sinatra on an open line to Sam's political fixers and to Democratic National Committee chairman Jake Arvey.

By midnight NBC News predicted that Nixon would win. Without Texas and Illinois, Kennedy could not make it. The mob had made sure that Kennedy would win, but he did so by only 9,400 votes in Illinois and with a final plurality of 118,000 votes out of 68 million; 80 percent in Sam's wards voted for Kennedy. Much later, in 1994, Evelyn Lincoln, Kennedy's secretary, admitted that the election had been bought. At the time of Kennedy's election, Giancana was on top of the world, believing that he would be happy for the next four years with Kennedy as president. Carlos Marcello, the don of New Orleans, handled the South to secure this election. Thus, other dons of the Mafia contributed to Kennedy's election, and none of them are known to have taken exception to Giancana's strong support of John F. Kennedy.

"If I can't be president, at least I can own one," Sam Giancana told his family. He knew, however, that he needed something more than his reputation for possible insurance in case of a double cross by the Kennedys. So to guarantee against a double cross, he called upon his old friend, Frank Sinatra, with whom he'd had a close relationship for nearly thirty years. Joe and Jack Kennedy had often visited the Cal-Neva Resort in the corner of California and Nevada. Giancana's daughter Antoinette revealed that in order to set up John F. Kennedy with women and get some blackmail material, Sam Giancana decided to buy the Cal-Neva Resort in Sinatra's name. The arrangement was that Sinatra was supposed to repay Giancana. Because Jimmy Hoffa owed Sam favors, it was wired from top to bottom by Hoffa's "bug boys."

Recently, Bob McDonnell, Sam's lawyer and Antoinette's husband, revealed that Sam had a contract out on Sinatra, who was not going to repay Sam the money for the resort. Only after two families from New York City came up with the money did Sam withdraw the contract to kill Sinatra.

According to Sam's brother Chuck, purchase of the Cal-Neva Resort was accomplished through the help of Bob Maheu, who had worked for many years in the CIA and later had his own private detective agency. At that time Sam was enjoying a large sapphire ring that Sinatra had given him as a token of their close relationship. One day John F. Kennedy was interrogating Giancana, treating him like a criminal before a Senate committee, and the next day he was meeting with him to get his backing.

In one of the Senate hearings Robert F. Kennedy had made the comment, "I thought that only little girls giggled, Mr. Giancana," after Sam had laughed at some of the questions from Bobby. Later Giancana said that he was laughing because he was remembering how John F. Kennedy behaved at the Cal-Neva Resort. He found it very funny that these hypocrites were pretending to be law-abiding citizens.

Giancana knew that Sinatra was introducing women to John F. Kennedy, including Marilyn Monroe. In January 1960 Giancana told Sinatra to work for Kennedy's election. Sinatra was willing because he had the idea that he could possibly be ambassador to Italy if Kennedy were elected. In a 1997 interview between author Seymour Hersh and Tina Sinatra, Frank's daughter, it was clear that Sam Giancana and Frank Sinatra had a number of meetings on golf courses and in restaurants to discuss Kennedy's election.

Details of a specific arrangement between Joe Kennedy and Sam Giancana for the 1960 election began with the help of William J. Tuohy, a highly respected judge of the Circuit Court of Cook County without any mob ties and a friend of Joe Kennedy. An appointment was set up between Joe Kennedy and Giancana with the aid of Robert J. McDonnell. A call came in the winter of 1959–1960 from Tuohy to McDonnell: "There is going to be a meeting with Joe Kennedy and Sam Giancana in my office."

McDonnell went to see Sam at the Armory Lounge in Forest Park, Illinois, which was often used as his headquarters, to convey the information. Giancana came to the Tuohy office with an associate, and the two of them sat down with Joe Kennedy after introductions by McDonnell, who then left with Judge Tuohy.

Later, Tuohy said, "I am glad that I was not privy to the conversation between Joe and Sam, because in my position, with my integrity, this favor that Joe has asked of me of setting up the meeting really repulsed me." Sam later said that he had enough dirt (including pictures) on John F. Kennedy and his father "to ruin ten political careers," so he felt safe with Joe Kennedy.

In a book published in 2001, *My Father's Daughter: A Memoir,* Tina Sinatra said that it was her father who was responsible for Joe Kennedy and Giancana's getting together. This book prompted us to explore this relationship further. Clearly, the major event was the introduction of Sam Giancana to Joe Kennedy by Robert McDonnell in Judge Tuohy's office. As previously mentioned, Sinatra and Giancana later had often met to discuss the upcoming presidential election.

Mobster Murray Humphreys's second wife, Jean, clearly indicated that she would not trust Joe Kennedy because he was a bootlegger during Prohibition and was well known by her husband, who called him a "four flusher" and a "double crosser." She claimed that he even hijacked his own liquor and sold it elsewhere repeatedly. Giancana, however, believed that cooperating with Joe Kennedy would result in the various congressional committees laying off the outfit, particularly the Chicago outfit. After Kennedy's election, Joe directed his son to appoint his brother as attorney general. When Senator Everett Dirksen of Illinois realized that this election had likely been stolen, he understood that any investigation of the election results would be directed by the attorney general, the president's brother, so he chose not to recommend such an investigation.

On February 7, 1960, at the Sands Hotel in Las Vegas, Sinatra introduced one of his former girlfriends, Judith Campbell, to John F. Kennedy because she looked very much like the senator's wife, Jacqueline. Giancana had told Sinatra that he also had wanted an introduction to Judith, and that took place in late March at the Miami Fontainebleau Hotel. Sam showered Campbell with gifts and used her as a go-between with Kennedy, a tenth link between the two. despite the fact that Sam and John both had intense emotional and physical relationships with Campbell, political and business relations also were involved. For example, in August 1962, Campbell's apartment was broken into by two brothers whose father had rented the getaway car. The father happened to be the chief of security of the General Dynamics Corporation. Three months later this same company was awarded by the Kennedy administration the $6.5 billion contract on the TFX fighter (F111); Congress was shocked by the award, which nearly everyone believed would be going to Boeing, that they investigated the matter up until the Kennedy assassination. This break-in to Campbell's apartment by family members from General Dynamics makes one wonder if this corporation used what they found to blackmail the president into making this controversial award. It is also conceivable that Kennedy could have used this corporation to clean up some dirty personal relationships or to remove implicating documents from Campbell's apartment.

Judith Campbell played a major role in the relationship between John F. Kennedy and Sam Giancana. In April 1960 Kennedy gave a large amount of money to Campbell to convey to Giancana; according to some individuals of the Giancana family the amount was $250,000. Four months later Kennedy asked that Campbell carry another satchel of money to Giancana and set up meetings between the two, especially in her bedroom. Other meetings between Kennedy and Giancana were set up by calls Campbell made for such arrangements. Before Kennedy's inauguration, a document was relayed by Campbell to Giancana regarding the possible assassination of Fidel Castro. Over the next year Campbell made more than ten trips to both Sam Giancana and mobster Johnny Rosselli with envelopes from Kennedy. Campbell made many trips between Washington DC and Chicago, handing documents to Giancana, then off to Las Vegas to give similar documents to Rosselli, and then to California and back to Washington DC. On April 28, 1961, Kennedy was to give a speech in Chicago and came to Judith's room in the Ambassador East Hotel for a few hours before the speech. Giancana came to the same room for a meeting with Kennedy.

Their last meeting was on August 8, 1961, in Washington DC. At that time a second woman was allegedly brought into the room for a sexual escapade, but Campbell was very upset with Kennedy for such an arrangement. Later, Sam Giancana came to the room for a meeting with the president. On that day, when Sam and JFK met in Campbell's room, the government installed microphones in the Armory Lounge in Forest Park, Illinois, to bug Giancana's favorite hangout. Kennedy, however, had always said, "Sam works for us," even though illegal bugs were now being placed to pick up information about Giancana.

According to author Seymour Hersh, former FBI agent William Carter said, "We considered Kennedy to be no better than Giancana or Rosselli" when it was known about his affair with Judith Campbell.

On February 27, 1962, J. Edgar Hoover sent a memo to Robert F. Kennedy, notifying him that he knew Campbell had been in contact with Johnny Rosselli and Sam Giancana and also had made two calls within that week to Evelyn Lincoln, the president's secretary. On March 22, 1962, Hoover had lunch in the White House and told the president "this was a dangerous sexual relationship" that the FBI had known about since the summer of 1960. In the next few months Judith Campbell continued to have many talks with Kennedy. There were at least ten phone calls from her to the White House during that time. Later, there was speculation that she was a go-between with California businessmen interested in defense contracts. In August 1962 Campbell ended her relationship with Kennedy. And by the fall of 1962 she was deeply involved with Sam Giancana. But she had become pregnant, allegedly by John F. Kennedy on their last visit, and that drove her to Giancana, who made an arrangement for an abortion at Grant Hospital in Chicago in January 1963. Giancana was very angry with Kennedy, who allegedly also wanted the abortion. Giancana proposed marriage, but Campbell refused since she believed Giancana was in love with his other girlfriend, the famous singer Phyllis McGuire.

Meanwhile, the CIA had contacted Giancana and mobsters Santos Trafficante and Johnny Rosselli to put together a plan to murder Castro. Sam's relationships with his mob associates were usually positive, especially with Rosselli. Whenever Antoinette met with these people, they had been either at the Giancana house, the Armory Lounge, Sam's Villa Venice nightclub in Wheeling, or various restaurants and hotels. Most of them acted like gentlemen around her, but a few, like Sam DeStefano, were crude in appearance and behavior. Her recollection of Johnny Rosselli was based on a number of meetings at the Fontainebleau Hotel in Miami Beach, Florida, especially when Frank Sinatra was appearing at that hotel. It was usual for Sam to meet Rosselli whenever he went to Florida. After Antoinette had met Rosselli on several occasions in Florida, she wondered what he was doing down there. Many years later, after the hearings of the 1975 Church Committee, she realized how deeply involved Rosselli and her father were in the attempt to assassinate Castro. One personal motivation for Giancana to eliminate Castro was the matter of the casinos and bars he owned in Havana before Castro took them over. Antoinette remembers that Rosselli always listened to her father, who was the leader of all conversations, especially about Cuba. Cuba was really important to Sam, since that was to be his "retirement." And another reason for Sam's concern was the fleet of shrimp boats also confiscated by Castro.

Giancana indicated that CIA director Allen Dulles had suggested the idea of killing Castro, and Richard Bissell (director of covert operations) and Sheffield Edwards (director of CIA office of security) had put the scheme into action. For a link between the CIA and the mob, they called upon Bob Maheu, who had contacts in both groups. For the training of troops to invade Cuba, Sam had designated Jack Ruby to help in supplying arms to Cuban exiles in Florida and Louisiana. The training of these troops was supervised mainly by Frank "Fiorini" Sturgis, formerly minister of games of chance in Havana, and Guy Banister. Banister had been in charge of the FBI in the Chicago area and had opened his own detective agency in New Orleans. Giancana's relationship to Kennedy's CIA in directing an attempted assassination of Cuba's Castro is the seventh link between Sam and Kennedy. But this CIA involvement meant that Giancana was likely setting up his own assassination in 1975.

As an example of the twists and turns of events at the time Giancana was working on the Cuba connection with the CIA, he convinced the agency to bug the home of entertainer Dan Rowan. He suspected Rowan was romancing his girlfriend, Phyllis McGuire. Arthur Balletti (some claim it was Edward DuBoise), Maheu's man, planted the bug but was caught. The FBI wanted to prosecute Giancana, who had engineered this operation, but the CIA's Sheffield Edwards persuaded the FBI to drop the charge. The CIA was not worried that the bug would make the Kennedys look bad, and they did it as a favor to Giancana.

When Sam learned that Robert F. Kennedy had been appointed attorney general, he felt that it was a rabbit punch in the dark. He sent mobster Louis McWillie to his Cal-Neva Resort in Lake Tahoe. McWillie had previously been the pit boss at the Tropicana Hotel in Havana, but now he was to spy on Robert F. Kennedy and his frequent casino romps. Sam later went to the White House for a private meeting with the president, during which he became suspicious of Kennedy's motives. Sam admitted it was a brilliant move on the part of Joe Kennedy to have his son made attorney general to cover up all of the dirty tricks that the Kennedys had played during and after the election. But now a Kennedy war against organized crime commenced.

Right after the election the president sent copies of confidential FBI memos for J. Edgar Hoover to Sam Giancana through Judy Campbell. Sam interpreted these memos to mean that he was in solid with the president after all and that FBI agents in Chicago who were tailing him at that time were only supposed to make it look good. But Robert F. Kennedy had compiled a list of leading mob bosses, and Sam Giancana's name was at the head of the list, a eighth example of a link between these two families. It looked like a perfect double cross.

On April 4, 1961, Giancana learned that mob boss Carlos Marcello had been deported to Guatemala; his worst fears were confirmed that the Kennedys were attacking their previous Mafia supporters. After the Bay of Pigs in Cuba, which was another disappointment for Sam, he calculated there was maybe at least one reversal of this negative trend. His former aide, Richard Cain of the Scalzitti family, was placed in a highly sensitive position, namely, chief of a special investigation unit of the Cook County Sheriff's Office. Sam viewed this as a secret victory.

On April 14, 1961, during the Bay of Pigs disaster, some bombers left Nicaragua, but they were less than half the number the CIA believed would be necessary for the invasion to succeed. They failed to wipe out the Cuban Air Force. A second air strike had been ordered and was ready to go, but was canceled by Kennedy. Fourteen hundred Cuban exiles were left vulnerable; more than a hundred were killed and a thousand were captured. On April 24 the president blamed the CIA, particularly director Allen Dulles, Director of Covert Operations Richard Bissell, and Deputy Director Charles Cabell. Kennedy vowed "to splinter the CIA into a thousand pieces" and later fired all three men. Cabell was said to have angrily denounced Kennedy as a traitor. Now the mob and rogue elements of the CIA shared a common enemy, namely, the president of the United States, John F. Kennedy.

By June 1961 the dreams of a cozy relationship with the Kennedy administration were crumbling for the mob. Mobster Murray Humphreys from Chicago became an unwelcome visitor in the Oval Office, and the Kennedys also snubbed Sinatra by refusing an invitation to his new Palm Springs estate. They also made clear that he was not welcome in the White House. The double cross was firmly in place since the word had come from Joe Kennedy to the Skinny D'Amato group at the Cal-Neva Resort that Robert F. Kennedy would not allow Joe Adonis back into this country, as had been promised before the West Virginia primary. The calls from Judith Campbell were also suddenly refused at the White House, and there were no more FBI reports routed to Sam. Robert F. Kennedy was busy trying to destroy the number-one boss of the mob, Sam Giancana, but no one had ever made a fool of Sam.

Giancana claimed at that time, "I am going to send a message they'll never forget." Daughter Antoinette remembers other statements he made. "Some day they are gonna get their lunch, in other words, somebody is gonna take after them and really destroy them, and it won't just be me, it's also going to be others that are going to lead to the Kennedy demise." She thought at first that this statement was rather unusual, for she didn't realize until later the great hostility that Sam had toward the two Kennedys.

In January 1963 a cry went out from the underworld coast to coast that Kennedy was to be eliminated, especially since the boss of all bosses, Sam Giancana, began receiving a great amount of heat from the FBI, as had Jimmy Hoffa and Carlos Marcello. In June 1963 there was increased surveillance of Sam by FBI agents Marshall Rutland and Bill Roemer, who would accompany Sam even to the men's room.

Sam's half brother Chuck indicated that the secret plan for the Kennedy assassination involved the mayor of Dallas, Earle Cabell, whose brother was former CIA Deputy Director Charles Cabell. Also, Chuck said that the three main Mafia chieftains sent as possible shooters their own representatives to Dallas. Carlos Marcello of New Orleans dispatched Charles Harrelson and Jack Lawrence; Santos Trafficante contributed two Cuban exile friends. Harrelson had previously killed five people and is now serving a life sentence. He agreed (in a television interview) that one of the hobos or tramps filmed in the Dallas railroad yard on November 22, 1963, looked very much like him. Sam sent Richard Cain, Chuckie Nicoletti, and Chuckie's most important soldier, Deadeye. "Milwaukee Phil" Alderisio was a backup but not a shooter. Sam Giancana later claimed that Cain, not Lee Harvey Oswald, had fired from the sixth-floor window. Some individuals, like Robert Blakey, chief counsel for the 1978 House Assassination Committee, claimed Cain was legally blind, but Antoinette Giancana remembers that he was a sharpshooter in the service and later had glasses to correct his vision. According to Sam's half brother, J. D. Tippit and Roscoe White were there to murder Oswald, but when Tippit wavered, he was killed by White. Giancana's contribution to the Kennedy assassination is the tenth and the ultimate link between John F. Kennedy and him.

Giancana said, "We took care of Jack Kennedy together" and "parts of the government and the outfit really were two sides of the same coin." Other examples of two sides of the same coin can be seen by the close relationships between members of the mob and the CIA. The mob was allegedly running guns for the CIA with the help of their own lieutenants, including Louis McWillie, previously a pit boss in Cuba. Jack Ruby of Dallas was friends with undercover agents, and gave the CIA operative and outfit pilot David Ferrie a job in his Carousel Club. Ruby had a good relationship with the Dallas Police, and because Oswald had knowledge of the whole arrangement, he could have blown the lid off the operation. All the outfit guys knew it was better to die in prison as a murderer than to die at the hands of vengeful Mafia enforcers for screwing up a job. To explain what happened to Oswald, it is important to realize that Jack Ruby understood that he dare not fail. Members of the mob had all remembered the case of Action Jackson in Chicago, who a few years before had been brutally tortured to death because it was believed he had ratted on the outfit.

There are other examples of two sides of the same coin, all related to the Mafia. Lee Harvey Oswald had been connected to the New Orleans mob, because his uncle, Charles "Dutz" Murret, was one of Carlos Marcello's lieutenants. Oswald had been part of the Civil Air Patrol in earlier years with David Ferrie, who was part of the New Orleans Mafia and also worked for the CIA. On the other hand, Oswald had training from the Office of Naval Intelligence, especially at his marine outpost at Atsuga, Japan. Sam had always said that Oswald was a CIA agent, even while he was in Russia; when he returned to the United States he was managed by the CIA through former FBI agent Guy Banister. Banister's office was on 544 Camp Street, the same address as on the leaflets Oswald had handed out in his Hands Off Cuba campaign. In Dallas, Oswald had befriended George DeMohrenschildt, who had helped the outfit a great deal through oil ventures since he had been an expert oil engineer.

According to the Giancana family, in the spring of 1963 a decision was reached by Sam and rogue elements of the CIA to finalize the plans for the assassination. Lee Harvey Oswald seemed a natural choice as the fall guy. For information they relied upon Johnny

Rosselli's meetings with Guy Banister, Robert Maheu, and former CIA deputy director Charles Cabell, who had later been employed in the Maheu Detective Agency. Rosselli met several times with CIA agent Frank "Fiorini" Sturgis. The entire conspiracy went right to the top of some governmental agencies. Sturgis was the same person who played a role in the Nixon Watergate fiasco. A similar situation involved Richard Cain, who was an outfit man but also was made chief of a special investigation unit under Illinois Cook County Sheriff Richard Ogilvie. Law enforcement and the outfit remained securely linked.

After the Kennedy assassination in November 1963, even with the removal of Robert F. Kennedy as attorney general, the Justice Department continued to target Sam Giancana. In May 1965 he was given immunity but refused to talk about the Mafia, so he was sentenced to Cook County Jail for contempt of court, staying there until Memorial Day 1966. Sam was then off to Mexico, appointing Teets Battaglia to be in charge of the Chicago group. Giancana claimed that he still had many partners within the CIA on his numerous deals throughout the world. He and Richard Cain made many trips to Latin America, the Middle East, and other places, including contacts with King Farouk of Egypt and the Shah of Iran, where casinos were set up. In the summer of 1967 Sandy Smith of *Life* magazine revealed that Giancana was living in Mexico.

Summary

Sam Giancana was likely the most powerful Mafia don in the country in the early 1960s and had poured millions of dollars into Havana's casinos and shrimp industry before losing it all during Castro's nationalization of most businesses. Sam's relationship with the Kennedy family goes back to the time he helped to save Joseph Kennedy from Frank Costello's wrath, but it took on a new dimension with the 1960 election, when Giancana helped Kennedy to buy his victory in return for promises of future cooperation from the White House. There are as many as fourteen links between the Chicago mob and the Kennedys, especially between Giancana and John F. Kennedy. The Kennedys' double cross is clearly evident, and all the many promises to Sam and the outfit were broken. Sam was directly involved in the CIA plan to murder Castro, and he was one of the many who blamed Kennedy for the Bay of Pigs disaster, allowing his millions in Cuba to be forever lost. His hatred toward the president was further intensified by the fact that his own girlfriend, Judith Campbell, was made pregnant, allegedly by Kennedy, and Sam had to arrange an abortion for her at Grant Hospital in Chicago. Giancana had great motivation to kill Kennedy and told his daughter Antoinette that the Kennedys "would get their lunch and it would not just be me." Later he added, "The outfit had taken care of them."

8

The Church Committee
Prelude to the
Giancana Assassination

W E HAVE INTRODUCED MANY interrelationships between John F. Kennedy and Sam Giancana. As a further discussion of the Giancana murder, we will provide further details of the workings of the 1976 Church Committee because Giancana's assassination can only be explained by the workings of the CIA in the 1960s and 1970s as they were revealed by this committee. In order to further discuss who killed Giancana, we must first examine the CIA-Mafia plot to kill Castro that occurred years before Giancana's death. If this CIA-Mafia plot had been widely known at the time of Giancana's murder, there would have been no reason to implicate the government or the mob for killing him to keep him quiet about these plans. On the other hand, if little were known by relatively few, and especially if the information would be very embarrassing to an agency that had murder as one of its stock tools of the trade, then there would be an understandable need to silence Sam. An important publication to address these concerns was the *Alleged Assassination Plots Involving Foreign Leaders* from the Senate Select Committee on Intelligence, chaired by Frank Church.

In the foreword to this publication, investigator Clark R. Mollenhoff states that 349 pages of the report include clear evidence and general conclusions by all members of the committee that leave little doubt that four presidents—Dwight D. Eisenhower, John F. Kennedy, Lyndon B. Johnson, and Richard M. Nixon—knew of and in some manner approved the plots undertaken. Those plots involved Chile's Rene Schneider, the Congo's Patrice Lumumba, Cuba's Fidel Castro, the Dominican Republic's Rafael Trujillo, and South Vietnam's Ngo Dinh Diem.

This report shows that the White House had a contract out on the life of Castro almost continuously, from 1960 throughout the Kennedy and Johnson administrations. The evidence that Kennedy knew a great deal about the Cuban plots comes from many different sources. For example, the command sergeant major of the Eighty-sixth Airborne, Clarence B. Sprouse, said that the CIA's Richard Bissell had briefed Kennedy in mid-1960 regarding Cuba. In addition, Kennedy was told of the Cuban plots in the fall of 1960 by John Patterson, who at that time was governor of Alabama. Six days before Kennedy's election, the CIA's Charles Cabell flew to California to brief him on the Cuban plots. Finally, CIA director Allen Dulles was well acquainted with Kennedy through Palm Beach, Florida, society and therefore would likely have shared information on the Cuban situation with him.

An example of an assassination that did occur, involving another head of state, was Ngo Dinh Diem, who was murdered in November 1963. In August 1963 the Kennedy administration had given approval for a military takeover. Gen. Duong Van Minh was the leader of the takeover plot, which would require that Diem be killed. The CIA was aware of Minh's plot; thus, by backing Minh and supporting the takeover, the agency contributed indirectly to the death of Diem.

Regarding the plot to kill Castro, there is no doubt that CIA officials worked with underworld figures Santos Trafficante, John Rosselli, and Sam Giancana. The Church Committee report referred to an unidentified close friend of Kennedy on page 129 whom others have identified as Judith Campbell, a West Coast party girl. The official committee report states: "Evidence before the committee indicates that this close friend of President Kennedy had frequent contacts with the president from the end of 1960 through mid 1962. FBI reports and testimony indicate that the president's friend was also a close friend of John Rosselli and Sam Giancana and saw them often during this same period of time."

The committee reported that U.S. government personnel, in conjunction with American underworld figures and Cuban refugees, plotted to kill Castro from 1960 to 1965. Another conclusion of the Church Committee was that the plots against Castro can be understood by considering earlier CIA attempts to remove the dictator: the 1961 Bay of Pigs invasion and Operation Mongoose in 1962. As evidence for the CIA action against the Cuban dictator, in August 1975, Castro gave U.S. Senator George McGovern a list of twenty-four alleged CIA attempts to assassinate him.

This story involves two sets of dates, one in the early 1960s and another in mid-1975, when these facts were made known by the Church Committee. The following is the sequence of testimony given to the committee in 1975. On May 30, 1975, an unnamed CIA support chief testified that he asked former FBI agent Robert Maheu to contact John Rosselli in the early 1960s and offer him $150,000 for Castro's assassination. The offer was approved by senior CIA officials; only six people knew of this project at that time. From testimony ten days later, on June 9, 1975, more evidence of the Castro operation was detailed by testimony concerning a conversation between CIA Deputy Director Richard Bissell and Director of Security Sheffield Edwards, briefing Director Allen Dulles. Bissell and Edwards discussed the need to find someone to kill Castro. Bissell told the committee that he believes Edwards said, "We need to contact members of a gambling syndicate operating in Cuba." Thus, before Sam Giancana was assassinated on June 19, 1975, only Bissell, Edwards, and the support chief had given brief testimony to the Church Committee of a general plan to kill Castro with the help of a gambling syndicate.

On page 77 of the Church Committee report is the first mention of "Sam Gold, who was really Momo Salvatore Giancana, a Chicago-based gangster." There is a footnote that "Sam Giancana was murdered in his home on June 19, 1975."

Johnny Rosselli's testimony occurred on June 24, after Giancana's death, and he described the sequence of events in the early 1960s. According to Rosselli, he and Maheu met at the Brown Derby restaurant in Beverly Hills in early September 1960, and then a meeting was arranged for the two of them with the CIA support chief at the Plaza Hotel in New York on September 14, 1960. The support chief arranged for Rosselli to go to Florida to recruit Cubans for part of this operation. Ten days later the three men met in Miami to work out the details of the operation. While in Miami, Rosselli introduced Maheu to two others who would work with him; one was called "Sam Gold," clearly Sam Giancana, the other was called "Joe," and he was Santos Trafficante. The committee report also included information based on the FBI's electronic bugging of conversations between Rosselli and Giancana. On the basis of this information, the FBI sent a night cable to their agents that there seemed to be a mob plot to kill Castro and to watch out for Giancana. Wherever Giancana went, particularly if he were to go to Miami, the FBI wanted to know who he contacted. One wonders if the FBI and the CIA were operating at cross purposes in dealing with the Giancana team being assembled to assassinate Castro.

Robert Maheu testified on July 29, 1975, that he had known Rosselli since the 1950s and that Giancana's job was to find someone in Castro's circle who could accomplish the assassination. Maheu met almost daily with Giancana for a long time. He said that Giancana was paid nothing, not even for expenses, and that Rosselli was given only a pittance that did not even begin to cover his expenses. Later testimony, however, revealed that Giancana and Rosselli did receive payment for their services. In late October 1960 Maheu arranged for Florida investigator Edward DuBoise to bug a room in Las Vegas, because Sam Giancana suspected his girlfriend, singer Phyllis McGuire, was having an affair with the entertainer Dan Rowan. But while Giancana wanted to find out if his girlfriend was cheating on him, Maheu wanted to find out if Giancana had told her anything about the assassination plot against Castro and if she was spreading this story.

On May 30, 1975, the CIA support chief gave testimony. Bissell and Edwards appeared before the committee on June 9, and Giancana's killing was ten days later, when very few details had been given to the Church Committee about the Castro plot and the Mafia's involvement. Rosselli testified later on June 24, and Maheu much later on July 29. The support chief had known Santos Trafficante and Sam Giancana only as Joe and Sam Gold and only later knew who they really were. Bissell and Edwards added only a few more facts. After Giancana's death, Rosselli gave some further details, but Maheu's testimony (forty days after Giancana's assassination) included most of the details of this arrangement with the two Mafia dons. Six days before Maheu's testimony, Senator George A. Smathers (D-FL) told the committee that he had tried to discuss Cuba with President Kennedy, but the president made it clear that Smathers should never raise the subject with him again and emphasized it so strongly that he cracked his dinner plate with a knife at the mention of Cuba.

Now, many years after the Church Committee's 1975 hearings, we can clarify the actual details of the sequence of events in the 1960s that make up this story. On December 11, 1959, CIA Director Dulles authorized a plan to eliminate Fidel Castro. In August 1960 the CIA's Bissell and Edwards discussed using underworld figures to aid in this assassination and in the following month briefed other major players in the CIA. In late September 1960 the first meeting between Rosselli, Maheu, and the CIA support chief took place. On October 18 FBI Director Hoover sent a memo to the CIA director that Sam Giancana seemed to be involved in a plot to assassinate Castro in November. After President Kennedy took office, but before the Bay of Pigs, the CIA's Richard Bissell and William Harvey had discussions about assassinations of foreign leaders.

The CIA's Harvey, according to testimony from both Bissell and Harvey, was given the job of setting up procedures by which foreign leaders could be assassinated. This action was given the euphemism "executive action" and referred to later by the cryptonym ZR-RIFLE. Harvey had a long background in secret activities and was head of a task force of the CIA called W, a part of the Kennedy administration's hidden efforts to oust Castro in any way. In Florida, Harvey asked for arms and equipment to train Cuban refugees with the help of the CIA's Miami radio station, which ran a secret operation against Cuba called JM-WAVE. Harvey said he had kept the CIA's Richard Helms (later director of the agency) informed of the operation involving the underworld at all stages. In mid-July 1975 Helms told the Church Committee he had reluctantly approved the operation, but he had no confidence it would succeed. Just before the Bay of Pigs invasion, Senator George A. Smathers raised the subject of Cuba at a dinner with President Kennedy and received a severe rebuke from the president not to mention it again. Also, at that same time, Rosselli passed some poison pills to a Cuban in Miami.

From April 15 to April 17, 1961, the Bay of Pigs invasion failed. The next day Maheu told the FBI of the CIA involvement in the wiretap of Dan Rowan. On May 7 CIA members met with Attorney General Robert F. Kennedy, and the decision was made to offer Rosselli and Giancana $150,000 to kill Castro. Bissell said he had no direct knowledge that Robert F. Kennedy knew of the plot to kill Castro, but he had briefed the attorney general on using the underworld against Castro. Just two days later Attorney General Kennedy told Hoover he was upset that the CIA had hired Maheu to approach Giancana about paying $150,000 for a gunman to kill Castro. Thus, by May 1961, Robert F. Kennedy and J. Edgar Hoover were well aware that the CIA was using Giancana in an operation against Cuba, specifically to kill Castro. However, Sam Halpern, executive officer of Task Force W, testified that the attorney general did not argue that the CIA should not utilize the mob in this endeavor but only that they should check with him before any further involvement.

On June 6, 1961, Courtney Evans, the FBI's liaison with President Kennedy and Attorney General Kennedy, sent a memo to FBI Assistant Director Ellen Belmont, indicating that the CIA had used Maheu as a go-between in contacting Sam Giancana, "the notorious Chicago hoodlum," in a plan to eliminate Castro. The CIA asked that this information be handled on a "need to know basis." These were some of the many interrelationships between the FBI, CIA, and Mafia, and the Evans memo is another example of the knowledge that the Kennedys had about Giancana and his assignment to kill Castro.

On November 16, 1961, President Kennedy gave a speech saying he was against assassination by any arm of the government, but three days later the CIA's Operation Mongoose was created as a covert action to overthrow Castro. A few months later, on January 19, 1962, at a Mongoose meeting, Robert F. Kennedy said that the solution to the Cuban problem was a top priority. Ten days later the CIA quashed the prosecution of anyone (especially Giancana) involved in the Las Vegas wiretap, and on February 19 Richard Helms succeeded Richard Bissell as deputy director of plans in the CIA. In late April 1962 Harvey passed poison pills to Rosselli in Miami, and on September 7 Rosselli told Harvey that the pills were in Cuba. In October Operation Mongoose officially ended, but even during the following year the CIA worked on exploding seashells and contaminated diving suits for Castro. On November 22, 1963, President Kennedy was assassinated.

Later the CIA AM/LASH program tried a poison-pen device for killing Castro. In 1966 new CIA Director Helms reported to Secretary of State Dean Rusk that the CIA was not then involved in the AM/LASH program or in any plot to assassinate Castro.

One conclusion of the Committee was that, although no foreign leader was killed as a direct result of a plot initiated by U.S. officials, the CIA knew about and encouraged two plots that resulted in the deaths of South Vietnam's Diem and Chile's Schneider. Another conclusion was that the United States should never again use underworld figures for political purposes. The assassination plots against Castro were clearly initiated by the CIA and approved by Director Allen Dulles, who was briefed by Bissell and Edwards about the underworld connection. Another conclusion was that in May 1961, Robert F. Kennedy and Hoover were aware that the CIA was trying to kill Castro by using Sam Giancana and other underworld figures. Perhaps the most important recommendation, still standing, until September 11, 2001, was that the United States must never engage in assassinations. The committee statement is signed by chairman Frank Church and committee members Howard Baker, Barry Goldwater, Gary Hart, Phillip Hart, Walter Huddleston, Charles Mathias, Walter Mondale, Richard Schweiker, John Tower, and Robert Vargan.

For more insight into the CIA and its plots, Senator Church's son, Forrester, has collected some very revealing information about his father and what the senator had uncovered in his book *Father and Son*. Senator Church thought that his single most important assignment during his twenty-four years in the Senate was his chairmanship of this Senate Select Committee on Intelligence. He realized that this was a political minefield and it would probably thwart any aspirations he had for the White House. He was also concerned that such an investigation could weaken the CIA and decrease America's global respect and power. Church said in May 1975, "It's not at all clear that the public will fully appreciate the need for the investigation of this kind." He added, "It's necessary for us to look very closely and critically at some of the activities of the CIA and FBI and other agencies."

Just before the Church committee began its investigation, Vice President Nelson Rockefeller was commissioned by President Gerald Ford to look into charges, first made in December 1974 by *New York Times* reporter Seymour Hersh, that the CIA had violated its charter by spying against antiwar activists during the late 1960s and early 1970s. Allegations also surfaced in the press about CIA involvement in assassination plots against Cuba's Castro, the Dominican Republic's Trujillo, and South Vietnam's Diem. When Rockefeller released his report, it included nothing about such assassination plots. Rockefeller claimed his commission did not have enough time to look into those charges and stated, "We didn't feel that we could come to a conclusion on partial information."

On April 7, 1975, the first day of the Rockefeller hearings, President Kennedy's former national security advisor, McGeorge Bundy, denied knowledge of any decision to assassinate a foreign leader. He feared perjuring himself, however, and went to the executive director of the Rockefeller Commission, David W. Belin, and said that he needed to refresh his memory. He then commented, "Oh, yes, I do recall 'executive action capability.'" In his 1997 book Seymour Hersh noted that Belin was angry because he knew that Bundy had lied and that both President Kennedy and Attorney General Kennedy had known about the Castro assassination plot. Bundy then went before the Church Committee in July 1975, after the CIA's Bissell and Harvey had been interviewed, found that his memory had improved, and said, "There was talk of murder in the White House" and the plan called ZR/RIFLE was for such an assassination.

Senator Church reported that he went to see Rockefeller, and it was one of the most beautifully finessed conversations he ever had. "My, how glad he was to see me. My, how honored he was with my visit. And when we asked him for all of the transcripts, he understood why we wanted them and agreed that it would help our hearings."

Church asked, "Will you give us the transcripts?"

Rockefeller said "no," and the vice president then published his report and told the American public that the CIA's sins were "not major."

Senator Church obviously disagreed. He claimed that both he and Rockefeller had all the hard evidence of the CIA assassination plots they needed. Church himself preferred the word *murder.*

The senator said, "I don't regard murder plots as a minor matter." In the last week of November 1975, the Church Committee released its findings on the CIA assassination plans.

From nearly ten thousand pages of sworn testimony, taken from more than one hundred witnesses over sixty days of closed-door hearings, the report outlined the CIA's assassination attempts against five foreign leaders. In addition to Castro, Diem, and Trujillo, the agency had also targeted Congo's Patrice Lumumba and Chile's Rene Schneider. Church said that the CIA was like a "rogue elephant" and that there was a very strong possibility of at least implicit authorization from the White House. The Church Committee found serious questions about the role of the CIA in the four overseas murders. In Vietnam the CIA had backed the group of generals who murdered Diem.

In December 1960 Lumumba was arrested and forced to leave his U.N. protection in the Congo and was immediately seized by opposition troops and taken to the Katanga Province, where he was murdered on January 17, 1961. Belgian officials engineered the transfer, and they kept CIA Chief Lawrence Devlin fully informed. The precise role of the CIA is not at this time known, but cables available to the Church Committee showed that the CIA's men in Africa understood that Lumumba would be murdered once he left the U.N. sanctuary. Therefore, the CIA was likely indirectly related to this murder. President Kennedy was not asked a single question about the death of Lumumba in a television news conference in 1961.

In December 1960 the Eisenhower administration had approved a plan of the CIA's Richard Bissell to supply anti-Trujillo forces in the Dominican Republic with weapons and bombs. In April 1961, during the Kennedy administration, a second set of weapons was sent to these forces, but after the failed Bay of Pigs invasion on April 17, further weapons were not provided. Trujillo was murdered on May 30, 1961, by troops who had received American weapons earlier that year. Thus, the CIA was at least indirectly involved in this murder. The State Department had ordered the CIA station to destroy all records concerning contacts with these troops. Later, the CIA said that the Kennedy administration was successful in the Dominican Republic by moving it from a totalitarian dictatorship to a Western-style democracy. Robert F. Kennedy expressed no concern whatsoever about the American role in Trujillo's murder.

In Chile, Gens. Robert Viaux and Camilo Valenzuela kidnapped Rene Schneider. He was shot on October 22, 1970, and died three days later. Since the CIA had backed the conspirators, this death can also be traced to the CIA. Thus, it seems very likely that the CIA played a role in the murders of Diem, Lumumba, Schneider, and Trujillo and also attempted to murder Castro.

Church was very concerned about other abuses within the CIA. These abuses of government power included the use of the Internal Revenue Service to gather information on American citizens simply because they disagreed with an administration. In addition, the CIA illegally accumulated seventy-two hundred files on American citizens because they disagreed with the prosecution of the Vietnam War. Finally, illegal mail-opening programs by the CIA were directed against Americans between 1940 and 1973. Finding his own file, Senator Church was surprised to discover a letter in that CIA file that he had written to his mother-in-law while he was in Moscow in 1971.

In 1976 Frank Church considered a run for the presidency, but at the last minute he decided not to run because Jimmy Carter seemed to be the probable nominee. When asked if he would consider the vice presidency, Church replied: "I have enemies in high places; I was on a committee that exposed corruption and wrongdoing. There are certain powerful board and conference rooms where I am friendless. I have played inquisitor, and inquisitors become critics. Do you know any wildly popular critics?" Later he said to his son he felt very naive and explained: "Just before we left Washington, I got a call from the CIA. They told me that they had received unconfirmed reports that the *Economist* magazine would be featuring an article in its October issue, revealing that my Senate Intelligence Committee had been infiltrated by the KGB. At the time I thought nothing about it. I know it was not true. The security could not have been tighter. Everyone on the committee received a top security clearance from the FBI. So I referred this matter to a member of the staff and thought nothing more about it." Church considered, "Can you imagine any rumor more certain to spook a Presidential candidate than that his prospective Vice President had overseen an operation which was infiltrated by the KGB?" He added, "They would not have to use it until it became clear that I was about to be chosen. Then, you can be sure that it would be part of the intelligence packet sent to Plains (Georgia) to Carter if it had not already been included." Of course, there was no article in the *Economist* magazine; there had been no KGB infiltration of the intelligence committee. The last person the CIA would want as vice president would be someone like Frank Church who had exposed abuses in the agency and would be a heartbeat away from the presidency.

Summary

The Senate committee chaired by Frank Church investigated CIA plans to assassinate four world leaders. Indirectly the CIA contributed to the deaths of Diem, Lumumba, Schneider, and Trujillo and major plans were under way to kill Castro with the help of the mob's Sam Giancana, Santos Trafficante, and Johnny Rosselli. Clear evidence indicates that Robert F. Kennedy and John F. Kennedy knew of and approved such plans, especially the plot against Castro. On November 24, 1998, tapes were released from the John F. Kennedy Library in which the president is heard to say that his administration must bear some responsibility for the assassination of South Vietnamese President Ngo Dinh Diem. The CIA's Operation Mongoose to remove Castro began in November 1961, lasted one year, and was supported and likely coordinated by Robert F. Kennedy. The earliest testimony before the Church Committee in 1975 was on May 30 by an unnamed CIA support chief who discussed the financial arrangements with the intended killers. The next testimony on June 9 was by the CIA Deputy Director Richard Bissell, who spoke of plans to use the mob and also reported sharing these plans with other CIA officials. Sam Giancana was killed on June 19–20, the day that Church Committee staffers arrived in Chicago to escort him to Washington DC. At that time very few details had yet been given about the plans to kill Castro. Later testimony by Johnny Rosselli on June 24 and by William Harvey on the next day added a few more details, which were clarified by Robert Maheu on July 29. Thus, at the time of Sam Giancana's murder, only a few details had been given to the committee, and it is reasonable to assume that the CIA would not want Giancana to testify. This agency had successfully plotted the death of four heads of state and would not be concerned about murdering a mob figure like Giancana. Johnny Rosselli later was murdered. As an example of the power and tactics of the CIA at that time, this agency essentially threatened Frank Church to make certain that he would not be a candidate for president or vice president of the United States.

9

The Mob Empire in Cuba and Harassment at Home

ONE OF THE REASONS why certain members of the Mafia despised President Kennedy was that he had "fouled up" the Cuban situation so that their great investments there were forever lost. The best way to relate this story is to examine Santos Trafficante. The life of Santos Trafficante Jr. is well documented by Frank Ragano, his lawyer, whose book was published in 1994 with Selwyn Raab. Trafficante's father, Santos Trafficante Sr., had come to the United States from Sicily in 1904, when he was eighteen years of age. Over the next twenty years Trafficante Sr. was a small-time robber and extortionist. Prohibition gave him great opportunities in the 1920s, but with the repeal of Prohibition in 1933, Trafficante Sr. turned his business from illegal booze to the game of boleta, which was introduced from Cuba. In the 1940s murder and intimidation were also part of the boleta business, and after World War II, Congress became interested in the Trafficante family. In 1951 a congressional committee headed by Estes Kefauver focused on Tampa, Florida, and the Trafficante family. And in May 1954 Santos Trafficante Sr. and thirty-four of his men were arrested in Florida for running the largest boleta ring in the country. The family later used its boleta profits to buy casinos in Havana.

The father and his five sons lived in Tampa, where on August 11,

1954, at the age of sixty-eight, Trafficante Sr. died of cancer. Trafficante Jr. ascended the throne. He was born Luigi Santos Trafficante on November 14, 1914. He owned the two largest casino operations in Havana and was closely associated with Meyer Lansky, the Mafia's financial wizard and banker. Lansky had spent a great deal of time in Cuba around 1957 and was the chief partner in three mob-financed Havana casinos, the largest of which was the Riviera. Trafficante Jr. was also involved in the Mafia Appalachian meeting of November 14, 1957, when all the Mafia chiefs met to discuss their plans, including the Cuban casinos. Later, Albert Anastasia of the mob was killed in New York City after a meeting there, where Trafficante opposed his attempted takeover of the Havana casinos. Trafficante had previously locked up control of Cuba's Hilton Casino, but he lost it when Anastasia was killed. Early in January 1958, District Attorney Frank Hogan of New York issued a warrant for Trafficante for questioning about the Anastasia murder, so Trafficante fled the country and moved to Cuba, though he occasionally slipped back into Tampa and Miami.

In 1957 Trafficante met Senator John F. Kennedy in Havana. Trafficante arranged for him to stay in a special suite at his Commadora Hotel with three prostitutes. Kennedy accepted the offer, and after viewing the activity in this suite through special mirrors, Trafficante lost all respect for him and considered him a rank hypocrite. Seymour Hersh in *The Dark Side of Camelot,* writes that while in Cuba, Kennedy had an affair with the wife of the Italian ambassador but stayed at the home of American ambassador Earl Smith and had an affair with his wife as well.

Trafficante enjoyed a lavish lifestyle in Havana. His father had begun the casino operations in 1946. He invested heavily in these operations and multiplied their profits after dictator Fulgencio Batista seized power in 1952. At that time Cuba was a playground for wealthy American tourists, and there was an especially large amount of action in the casinos.

In 1958 Trafficante and Giancana had the largest gambling network in Havana, all of which was legal. The nightclubs included San

Souci, the Capri, Dora Deauville, and Sevilla Biltmore. In December 1958 Trafficante invited attorney Frank Ragano to come to Havana for a New Year's Eve gala. When Ragano asked about Castro, Trafficante assured him that he was going nowhere and not to worry about him. But on New Year's Eve, Batista fled Cuba, and Castro's troops occupied the capital. Rioters burst into six of Havana's thirteen casinos. Trafficante's Capri, Deauville, and Sevilla Biltmore casinos were devastated; only the Commadora and San Souci were spared. Castro ordered the casinos closed, and overnight Trafficante's casino empire disappeared.

Trafficante did not consider fleeing Cuba, because he believed that Castro could not remain in office for long, especially when there were no tourists and most of the establishments were shut down. All employees were laid off. Soldiers awakened Trafficante one night, demanding that the employees be returned to work and be paid. For two months fifty musicians played nightly and chorus girls and waiters stood around with nothing to do because there were no customers. The military order had to be followed.

Trafficante's freedom ended on June 8, 1959, when he was declared an undesirable alien and deported. Trafficante, however, was sent to Trescornia immigration station, a prison in Havana.

His daughter, Mary Jo, had always wanted a wedding in Havana, and even though Trafficante was a prisoner, Castro furloughed him to attend his daughter's wedding. Trafficante attended the ceremony, but he was carefully guarded and later escorted back to Trescornia. Soon he was on an execution list and scheduled to die. Someone called Charles said that he could free Trafficante, because he had once saved Castro's life. This individual was also called Phantisimo for he was a mysterious character. He came to Trescornia with two Cubans and had Trafficante's name removed from the execution list; he claimed that Trafficante had paid him fifty-five thousand dollars to do so. But Charles was a con man, and he and Trafficante were soon on the death list again.

The charges against Trafficante included drug trafficking. When authorities were asked for evidence of Trafficante's drug trafficking, it was explained that his name meant exactly that—"dealer." Lawyer Frank Ragano appealed to the Ministry of Justice that although the name meant dealer, it was no indication that Trafficante was dealing drugs. On August 18, 1959, Trafficante was on his way back to Miami after some bribes were paid to secure his release.

The Cuban Revolution had cost Trafficante more than $20 million in hotels and casinos, which were taken over by Castro's communist government.

In the 1960 election, Trafficante voted for Nixon as a "realistic conservative politician who would not be hard on me and my friends." He had a bad opinion of John F. Kennedy from his time in Cuba and had as much contempt for Robert F. Kennedy for harping on law and order, which he viewed as cheap political pandering. Trafficante also was upset at Robert F. Kennedy for his behavior as chief council of the Senate Select Committee on Improper Activities in Labor and Management Field. Another of his complaints was that Robert F. Kennedy had been unfair to Jimmy Hoffa in his severe questions during the Senate Permanent Subcommittee on Investigation, which was chaired by John L. McClellan. That committee dealt with graft and mismanagement in unions. John F. Kennedy had also been a member, and Robert F. Kennedy, as chief council on that committee, really went after Hoffa, who was finally acquitted of bribery charges, but only after vicious harassment by the Kennedys. Robert F. Kennedy had tried to link Hoffa with Red Dorfman, a member of the Capone gang in Chicago, later linked to Sam Giancana. Robert F. Kennedy then started to put a special squeeze on the Mafia, especially on Santos Trafficante and Carlos Marcello, the two main Mafia leaders in the South who were close friends and now were very much under scrutiny by the U.S. attorney general.

Marcello indicated that he, Hoffa, and Trafficante were due for hard times as long as Robert F. Kennedy was in office. Their feeling was that this Robert F. Kennedy talked about law and order, but the Kennedys had made their fortune through bootlegging, so "somebody ought to kill those SOBs." Trafficante could not forget the picture in

Cuba of John F. Kennedy with the prostitutes, and he had no respect for Kennedy for engaging in this type of activity.

At one meeting with Robert F. Kennedy, Trafficante's friend Hoffa arrived on time, but Kennedy arrived late. A heated argument developed, which resulted in Hoffa trying to choke Kennedy, claiming that he was "going to kill him." His hatred toward Kennedy peaked in July 1963, when Hoffa said to attorney Frank Ragano that something had to be done and that the time had come for his friends, Santos Trafficante and Carlos Marcello, to take drastic actions to kill John F. Kennedy. Ragano did pass on the message to Trafficante and Marcello that Hoffa definitely wanted to get rid of the president. Hoffa later made a point of asking Ragano if he had delivered the message.

Ragano replied, "Yes, Jimmy, I delivered the message."

After the president's murder, Santos Trafficante felt like "a load of stones was lifted off my shoulders. Now they'll get off my back and off Carlos and Jimmy." His hope was that the mob would get back to Cuba and would be making big money again. Lyndon B. Johnson was now in the White House, and he was certainly going to remove Robert F. Kennedy from any position of authority.

Just after the assassination, Trafficante and Ragano raised their glasses, and Trafficante toasted to one hundred years of health and to the death of John F. Kennedy. In August 1964 Robert F. Kennedy resigned as attorney general. For Trafficante and most of the Mafia dons the mid-1960s were a quiet, peaceful period. In 1967 Trafficante reported to Ragano that the CIA again wanted help in killing Castro, so the agency got in touch with Sam Giancana and Johnny Rosselli and later came to him. Rosselli had been very excited by this request, because the government had been trying to deport him for years, and if he could do this, they wouldn't deport him and would leave him alone. Not only would they leave him alone, but the Justice Department would back off from the mob if they did this favor for the CIA.

The CIA provided some pills to kill Castro, but Trafficante said he just flushed them down the toilet. Also, he claimed that in the early 1960s the CIA paid a lot of money to the mob, but neither he nor

Giancana nor Rosselli really intended to do anything about assassinating Castro. Speculation was that Giancana made certain that no assassination could occur before the 1960 election. Castro's death could only give a boost to Nixon and hurt Kennedy's chances for election, which the mob was supporting. The exploding cigars for Castro were not delivered until February 13, 1961, three weeks after the Kennedy inauguration and never were sent to Cuba. Robert Maheu had been the middleman between the CIA and the mob, since he had many connections with the mob through his former job as an FBI agent and later as a private detective.

Up to that time Ragano had believed that the CIA was strictly a law-enforcement agency and an enemy of the Mafia. Trafficante's tale of international intrigue, however, shows that the government was willing to use the mob for its political purposes. Months after Kennedy's assassination, Giancana joined Trafficante and Ragano and said, "We broke our balls for John F. Kennedy and gave him the election, and he gets his brother to hound us to death."

In 1960 Ragano had sued *Time* magazine for libel after they published his photo with members of the mob, suggesting that he was part of the Mafia. For this case, which came to trial after the 1963 Kennedy murder, Ragano enlisted famous San Francisco lawyer Melvin Belli as his attorney. Trafficante said to Ragano, "Whatever you do, do not ask Melvin Belli about his previous client, Jack Ruby." Ragano's confidence in Trafficante was unshakable, and the notion that Trafficante might be implicated in the Kennedy assassination was at first too far-fetched for him to consider. But what was the implication for advising him not to ask Belli anything about Ruby?

Meanwhile, the CIA had offered $150,000 to the potential assassins of Castro, and Robert Maheu had delivered the poison pills and $10,000 in cash in early 1961. This occurred at the Fontainebleau Hotel in Miami where Rosselli, Trafficante, Giancana, and a fourth man, a Cuban exile, met. In testimony before the Church Committee, Rosselli had recalled a session in late 1960 or early 1961, before the Bay of Pigs invasion, in which Maheu opened some briefcases, dumped a lot of money into his lap, and handed over capsules that were to be used in boiling soup or water as a way to get rid of Castro. Trafficante confided to Ragano in 1967 that they had outwitted and swindled the government by pretending to arrange for the hit on Castro. Instead they just pocketed the CIA cash. Although CIA officials claimed that the mobsters never made a cent from these arrangements, the testimony of Trafficante to Ragano of some financial benefits is more believable.

Ragano had theorized that the murder of Sam Giancana was a CIA job to prevent him from talking about the CIA/Castro plot. Then on August 7, 1976, a fifty-five-gallon oil drum was fished out of Dumfoundling Bay in North Miami; it contained the body of Johnny Rosselli. It was determined that Rosselli had been strangled and suffocated. Speculation was that both the Giancana and the Rosselli murders were related to the proposed Castro assassination, but there was no solid evidence. The fact that Trafficante was the sole survivor of these three mobsters recruited by the CIA to kill Castro is no evidence that Trafficante was responsible for either or both murders.

In 1979 a report of the U.S. House of Representatives Assassination Committee, by itself, did not convince Ragano that Trafficante and Marcello were implicated in John F. Kennedy's death, even though the report emphasized that in September 1962 Trafficante had told associate Jose Aleman that Kennedy would be hit. But on March 13, 1987, while dying of cardiological and renal problems, Trafficante confessed to Frank Ragano: "Bobby [Kennedy] made life miserable for me and my friends. The biggest mistake of my life was not taking pictures of the president when he was in Cuba and that was a bad mistake. I think Carlos Marcello screwed up in getting rid of John F. Kennedy; maybe it should have been Bobby." In Ragano's opinion, Trafficante confessed that he and Carlos Marcello had conspired to kill the president. Ragano realized that he had unwittingly suppressed for more than two decades facts that could no longer be ignored. In Ragano's opinion, Carlos Marcello, Santos Trafficante, Sam Giancana, and Jimmy Hoffa played important roles in President Kennedy's death.

Ragano also pondered Hoffa's murder. After Hoffa had been jailed, the new Teamsters head, Frank Fitzsimmons, was easier to control by the Mafia than Hoffa, who had his own ideas. When Hoffa was released from prison, he disappeared on July 30, 1975, and was killed on the order of Anthony "Tough Tony" Provenzano, who hated Hoffa, especially after a fight with him when they were both in prison. Sal Briguglio and his brother, Gabriel, worked for Provenzano. Tommy Andretta put a rope around Hoffa's neck and choked him to death. In March 1978 "Sally Buggs" was gunned down in New York's Little Italy, and later that year Tony "Pro," Gabe Briguglio, and Tommy Andretta were sentenced to long prison terms for labor racketeering.

In March 1987 Santos Trafficante, after meeting with Frank Ragano, was flown to the Texas Heart Institute and died there two days later, on March 17, 1987, at the age of seventy-two, when he failed to survive a heart bypass operation. Trafficante had a Machiavellian reason for confessing to the crime of the century, the conspiracy to assassinate John F. Kennedy. His admission did not violate his private code of morality, his oath of *omerta,* because he was not giving the information to a law-enforcement agent about someone in the mob, and therefore he was not harming any living person. Carlos Marcello was suffering from Alzheimer's disease, and Sam Giancana was dead. Trafficante had a perverse pride that he and the mob had eliminated the president, outwitted the top government law-enforcement agencies, and escaped punishment. Joe Kennedy had made a commitment for his sons, which they had violated by reneging on their part of the bargain. Thus the Kennedys were fair game. If there had been no bargain between the Kennedys and the mob, it is quite possible John F. Kennedy would be alive today. Furthermore, Trafficante despised Kennedy for withholding air support from the anti-Castro forces in the 1961 Bay of Pigs invasion, dooming the counterrevolution. With the elimination of Castro after a successful Bay of Pigs operation, John F. Kennedy would have cleared the way for Trafficante and other mobsters to make a glorious comeback in Havana.

The message that Ragano delivered from Hoffa to Trafficante in July

1963 to kill Kennedy had probably not started the plot, but it added to it, for the lawyer realized the mob had already been planning the hit. Days after the assassination, Hoffa said to Ragano, "I told you they could do it." Two weeks after the assassination, Carlos Marcello and Santos Trafficante were joking about the assassination and said that Hoffa owed them "big." Ragano wrote his book when he was seventy-one years old and his health was failing from a heart attack and bouts of angina. At the end of his life, Ragano felt compelled to reveal what he knew of how the Mafia arranged for the death of the president.

Summary

Santos Trafficante was the don of Florida but also owned many casinos and hotels in Havana. His empire disappeared when Castro took over Cuba, and he lost more than $20 million. Trafficante was scheduled by Castro to be executed when bribes allowed for his escape. He had a special interest in killing Castro when he, Sam Giancana, and Johnny Rosselli were "hired" to do the job for the CIA, but those plans failed. He hoped that the Bay of Pigs invasion would eliminate Castro and that he could revive his casino-hotel empire, but President Kennedy thwarted the invasion by halting the departure of aircraft that would have assured victory for the Cuban rebels. His anger toward Kennedy was further increased by Kennedy's treatment of Jimmy Hoffa, who appealed to him and Carlos Marcello to get rid of the president. A dying Trafficante confessed to his friend and lawyer Frank Ragano that Robert F. Kennedy had made his life miserable and that he despised John F. Kennedy for the Bay of Pigs fiasco. Thus Santos Trafficante was motivated to eliminate the president and confessed to his lawyer about the conspiracy to kill Kennedy.

10

Harassment by the Kennedys

A STRONG MOTIVATING FORCE to kill John F. Kennedy was the unrelenting harassment of the mob, especially by Attorney General Robert F.
Kennedy. The best example of the lengths to which Robert F. Kennedy
was determined to go is the case he pursued against Carlos Marcello.

Marcello was born on February 6, 1910, and arrived in Louisiana
eight months later with his mother, Luigia Minacore. She joined her
husband, Giuseppe, who had arrived the year before on the Italian
liner *Liguria*. They were scheduled to work on the North sugar plan-
tation where an overseer was also named Minacore, so they were
given the names Joseph and Louise Marcello, and their son, Calogaros, was called Carlos. Carlos had actually been born in Tunis but was
not naturalized. The Marcellos then traveled to New Orleans and
went into the vegetable business. At nineteen, Carlos robbed a bank
of seven thousand dollars, which led to a sentence of from nine to
twelve years in the state penitentiary.

On May 28, 1930, at the age of twenty, he was given early release.
He then opened a liquor store and at age twenty-five was inducted
into the New Orleans Mafia, which was run by Sam "Silver Dollar"
Carolla. Carlos then married Jackie Todaro, the daughter of underboss
Frank Todaro.

Frank Costello from the New York mob had taken over the slot-machine business in New Orleans, and Carlos Marcello used his own Jefferson Music Company for their distribution. This company was set up in 1938 by Carlos and his brother Vincent. When Costello was ready to expand from the French Quarter to the West Bank, Carlos agreed that his music company would install and service the 250 slot machines for a fee—two-thirds of the gross. In 1947 the two brothers were building up the business to include services to racetrack gamblers. Marcello then became a big-timer as a casino owner and was considered by many to be a man of authority in the early 1940s. At the young age of thirty-eight, Carlos became the boss of the Louisiana Mafia. On January 25, 1951, he was summoned before Estes Kefauver's Special Committee to Investigate Organized Crime in Interstate Commerce for illegal gambling in Louisiana. He was their main witness.

In 1953 Marcello bought the Town and Country Motel to use as his new headquarters, and in the mid-1950s he also purchased the sixty-four-hundred-acres Churchill Farms, which he used for meetings. In 1959 the Senate Committee on Investigation of Corruption in Labor and Management was headed by Senator John L. McClellan, with Robert F. Kennedy as chief counsel. Aaron Kohn, head of the New Orleans Crime Commission, testified that Carlos Marcello had committed a litany of crimes, recited to Kennedy, including two murders. Marcello had long been suspected of masterminding most of these crimes, and so Kennedy announced, "We will do something about Mr. Marcello; we cannot permit this kind of corruption to exist in the U.S." In his testimony in front of the committee Marcello declined to answer any questions. Pierre Salinger, a staff investigator (later press secretary for John F. Kennedy), was called to testify to the truth of Kohn's assertions. He also grilled Marcello, and again Marcello declined to answer any questions, including whether he had U.S. citizenship. Kennedy remembered Marcello's arrogance and on March 24, 1959, asked the attorney general why deportation against Marcello had not proceeded. The Justice Department had been aware of a forged Guatemalan birth certificate for Calogaros Minacore, which had been obtained by Marcello through bribes of Guatemalan officials.

Robert F. Kennedy never forgot Marcello's defiance before the Mc-Clellan Committee. When he became attorney general after his brother's election, Robert F. Kennedy decided to use the fake Guatemalan birth certificate to deport Marcello. At first he intended to deport him to Formosa or Taiwan but eventually deporting him to Guatemala.

Attorney General Kennedy ordered Marcello's expulsion on March 15, 1961. On the morning of April 4, as a routine sign-in, Marcello and one of his attorneys went to the immigration office in New Orleans and were told to wait. Generally, deportees signed in and left. A letter was delivered to Marcello informing him that he was to be sent to Guatemala. Accompanied by his lawyer, Marcello was handcuffed, taken to a car, and hustled to the New Orleans International Airport. A plane was waiting for him, but he was not allowed to phone either his wife or his primary attorney, Jack Wasserman. Of course, Marcello was furious with Robert F. Kennedy not only for this treatment but also for the grilling he withstood before the McClellan Committee.

When he arrived at the military airport in Guatemala City, Marcello was met by a colonel who asked him where he wanted to go. Marcello asked to be taken to a hotel, but the colonel's secretary invited him to stay at her apartment that first night. Marcello suspected this was a setup, so he got no sleep that night. The next day he was sent to jail, but he bribed his way out with seventy-five thousand dollars and finally went to the Biltmore Hotel. Later, a station wagon removed him from Guatemala City to an El Salvador army camp in the jungle. Accompanying him was one of his attorneys, Mike Maroun from Shreveport, Louisiana. Both of them were placed on a bus and driven for six hours twenty miles into Honduras, where they were marooned. There was no civilization in sight and very little to eat or drink, and Marcello had significant difficulty breathing at the high altitude. For two days and nights Marcello and Maroun struggled to remain alive, trying to walk down to the Honduran plains. By the time they reached their goal Marcello had broken three ribs and was in great pain, but he finally made it to a provincial airport.

Marcello and Maroun then flew to the Honduran capital, Tegucigalpa, and registered at a hotel where Marcello slept for two days. He was eager to get back to New Orleans, and there is some question as to how he accomplished that. Some evidence suggests he traveled first to the Dominican Republic on a DR air force jet, courtesy of Rafael Trujillo. Then he made it to New Orleans, possibly flown there by David Ferrie, a former Eastern Airlines pilot who worked for both the mob and the CIA. On June 2, 1961, attorney Maroun announced to the press that Marcello was in hiding in Louisiana.

Three days later Attorney General Kennedy dispatched twenty federal agents to Shreveport to pick up Marcello, since it was Maroun's hometown. Marcello later surrendered to immigration agents in New Orleans. By July 11 INS declared Marcello an illegal alien and again ordered his deportation, but an appeal by his attorney resulted in his being released in New Orleans.

Attorney Jack Wasserman filed a lawsuit against the attorney general for Marcello's illegal deportation to Guatemala, *Carlos Marcello v. Robert F. Kennedy*. On December 10, 1961, Marcello was freed on a ten-thousand-dollar-bond, but an appeal to the board of immigration upheld the deportation order. Evidence exists that Marcello contacted Angelo Bruno, the Mafia chieftain in Philadelphia, to ask Santos Trafficante and Sam Giancana to persuade Frank Sinatra to intervene on his behalf. Sinatra was to convince Robert F. Kennedy and Joseph Kennedy to lay off Marcello, but this action could only have made things worse at that time because Sinatra was no longer close to the Kennedys. And Robert F. Kennedy was more determined than ever to get Carlos Marcello.

A strategy meeting was held at Churchill Farms in the summer of 1962 between Marcello and associate Edward Becker. Becker understood that Marcello had been severely treated by Robert F. Kennedy, and Becker heard Marcello say, "If you want to kill a dog, you don't cut off its tail, you cut off its head." John F. Kennedy was the head,

Robert F. Kennedy was the tail. Robert F. Kennedy would lose all power if John F. Kennedy were killed; Lyndon B. Johnson would be president, and he hated Robert F. Kennedy. Johnson would reduce him to "just another lawyer."

In October 1962 Marcello's attorney tried to set aside Marcello's 1938 conviction for selling marijuana, since such a federal crime would justify deportation. But on October 31, 1962, the Supreme Court refused to hear the case. Early in January 1963, Robert F. Kennedy indicated to J. Edgar Hoover that the FBI should step up its actions against Marcello. But on May 27 the Supreme Court refused to review the deportation orders, which increased the pressure on Robert F. Kennedy.

To help in the defense against deportation, David Ferrie was retained by Marcello. Ferrie came to Marcello's attention through his other attorney, G. Wray Gill. This same attorney had represented Ferrie against Eastern Airlines when this company had fired him for overt homosexuality. Ferrie had also worked with former FBI special agent Guy Banister at 544 Camp Street, the same address used by Lee Harvey Oswald when handing out the pamphlets on Fair Play for Cuba.

On September 25, 1963, mobster Joseph Valachi testified before the McClellan Committee about how important the Mafia was throughout the country. Now there was even greater pressure on Trafficante, Giancana, and Marcello, because not only had organized crime, the Mafia, been exposed but many of its inner workings had been revealed. The trial of *U.S. v. Marcello* had been scheduled for early November 1963.

The Justice Department's case against Marcello was complicated the fact that Robert F. Kennedy had submitted a forged Guatemalan birth certificate as justification for his deportation to Guatemala. On November 1, 1963, there was a final showdown in the case of *U.S. v. Marcello*. And on November 21 the defense rested, with closing arguments on the very day that John F. Kennedy came to the Dallas–Fort Worth area. The verdict on November 22 was an acquittal for Marcello. On November 23 the *New Orleans Times-Picayune* had as its main headline that Carlos Marcello was found not guilty, and underneath that was the headline about the killing of President Kennedy and the wounding of Governor Connally.

Information gained by the 1975 Church Committee on CIA activities led to the 1976 House Committee on Assassination, which then drew important conclusions about Carlos Marcello. The Senate committee, chaired by Frank Church, was the first to reveal the dirty secrets of the CIA and the Mafia plot to murder Castro. John F. Kennedy had clearly ordered the CIA to kill Castro, and he and his brother had given their approval for a plot, called the AM/LASH plan, against Castro in 1963. According to a 1988 television interview with Judith Campbell, the president was clearly aware of the CIA-Mafia plot, and the Church Committee found that this plot had never been reported by the FBI, CIA, or Robert F. Kennedy to the Warren Commission. This same committee discovered the affairs between Campbell and John F. Kennedy and between Campbell and Sam Giancana. These discoveries led to a subcommittee study of the relationship of the FBI and CIA to the John F. Kennedy assassination, resulting in a collapse of the public's faith in the Warren Report. Senators Richard Schweiker and Gary Hart reportedly found that the FBI and the CIA had misled the Warren Commission to prevent the truth about the assassination from coming to light. The Church Committee found that one very important witness had been murdered a few days before he was to testify—Sam Giancana.

Johnny Rosselli was the next to die. Rosselli met with Schweiker and other committee members in the Carroll Arms Hotel in Washington DC. He indicated that he had good reason to believe that Cuban associates of Castro and Trafficante were involved in the Kennedy assassination and that he would testify to these facts. Ten days after a dinner with Santos Trafficante, Rosselli was murdered, presumably on a yacht belonging to a Trafficante associate; his dismembered body was dumped into the ocean in an oil drum. Hoffa also had been murdered, disappearing on July 30, 1975, although he was not scheduled to testify before the Church Committee.

WHAT WE KNOW: On November 22, 1963, President John F. Kennedy and Texas Governor John Connally (*above*) were shot in Dallas. The president died as a result of his wounds. Lee Harvey Oswald was apprehended and charged with the shooting. Oswald was killed (*below*) on November 24 by Jack Ruby.

WHAT WE HAVE UNCOVERED: This are photos of the real assassin, James Files, at age eleven (*above left*), age twenty-one (*above right*), and as he was photographed in the Lamplighter Motel in Mesquite, Texas, by Lee Harvey Oswald.

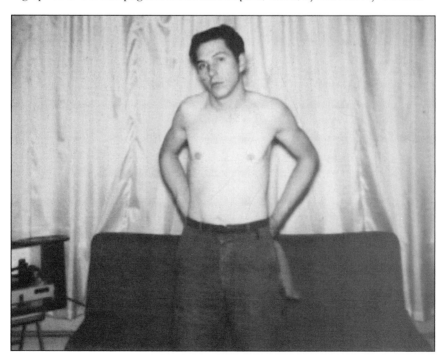

From the grassy knoll in front of the presidential limousine, Files shot Kennedy with a Remington Fireball XP-100 (*above*), a handgun with a telescopic sight, using exploding, fragmenting bullets.

Right: Files at age thirty-four.

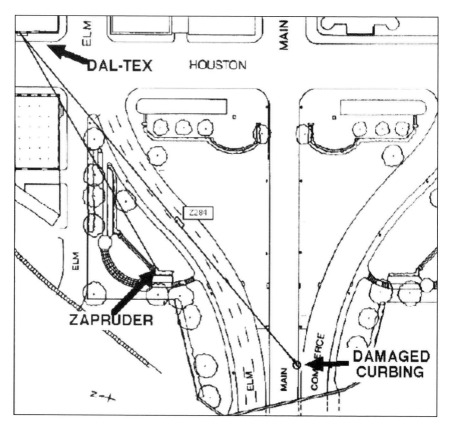

In the above sketch of Dealey Plaza, the scene of the assassination, the Dal-Tex Building is in line with the shots that struck Kennedy from behind. The middle arrow highlights the position from which Abraham Zapruder filmed the shots that struck the motorcade. The bottom right arrow points to where a shot struck the curbing; it also aligns with the Dal-Tex Building.

Shooting positions are marked on this photograph of Dealey Plaza: Chuckie Nicoletti and Johnny Rosselli in the Dal-Tex Building and James Files at the grassy knoll.

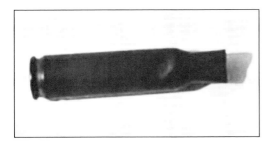

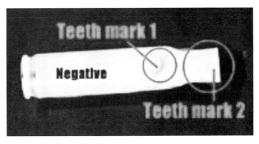

While digging near a fence line in Dealey Plaza in 1987, John C. Rademacher (*below*) unearthed a shell casing (*above*) that corroborates Files's claim that he bit the cartridge of the bullet he fired at Kennedy from the grassy knoll.

As part of their investigation into the Kennedy assassination, private investigator Joe West (*left*) and producer Bob Vernon (*right*) filed a lawsuit to exhume the president's body.

West's research led him to Jim Files (*left*), and the two were photographed together on August 16, 1992.

James Files is currently incarcerated at the Illinois State Penitentiary.

Files's March 22, 1994, interview is entitled *Confessions of an Assassin*. He details his connection with several members of the Giancana mob as well as his role in the aborted Bay of Pigs invasion. He arrived in Dallas a week before the president and was shown around town by Lee Harvey Oswald. On the day of the

assassination, Files drove Chuckie Nicoletti and Johnny Rosselli to the Dal-Tex Building. Two hours prior to Kennedy's arrival, Nicoletti asked Files to be one of the shooters and gave him a choice of weapon and position. Files chose the grassy knoll. Afterward he walked to his car and picked up Nicoletti and Rosselli and drove away.

Above: Sam Giancana and his wife, Angeline, and their daughter Antoinette.

Facing page: Sam Giancana and his wife, Angeline.

Sam Giancana and daughter Antoinette

Sam Giancana with assistant Tony Demarco

Sam Giancana between two members of the 42 Gang: "Fat Leonard" Caifano (*left*) and Joe Mundo (*right*).

Sam Giancana as a young man.

Antoinette Giancana as a glamorous "Mafia princess."

Antoinette Giancana as she appeared in *Playboy* in 1988. [Reproduced by Special Permission of Playboy Magazine. Copyright © 1988 by Playboy. Photo by Pompeo Posar.]

Sam Giancana at home.

The sudden deaths of Sam Giancana and Johnny Rosselli and the alleged heart attack of the CIA's William Harvey, the official in charge of the CIA-Mafia plot against Castro, helped to stimulate the formation of a committee to reinvestigate the Kennedy assassination. The Ninety-fourth Congress on September 1976 put together the House Select Committee on Assassinations to reinvestigate the John F. Kennedy and Martin Luther King assassinations. The committee's final report indicated that Carlos Marcello had "probable complicity above all others."

There were many examples of a relationship between Marcello and the major players in the assassination. Next to New Orleans, the most important city in Marcello's criminal empire was Dallas. Marcello had placed many slot machines throughout Texas, including in Dallas. Running the Dallas operation was Louisiana-born Joseph Civello, a friend of Marcello. Both were raised in Louisiana, both were Sicilian by birth, and both went into the Mafia early in their lives. Nightclub owner Jack Ruby had been close friends with Civello in Dallas and also with both Joe and Sam Campisi, owners of another Dallas nightclub. Lee Harvey Oswald also had a relationship with Marcello. Oswald's uncle was Dutz Murret, a member of the Marcello group. Oswald's mother also had ties to two associates of Marcello, and Oswald was once bailed out of jail by Emile Bruneau, a close associate of a Marcello aide. One more example of the interrelationship between the New Orleans and Dallas mobs is that Joe Campisi was Jack Ruby's first visitor in prison.

The evidence that Carlos Marcello was likely involved in the assassination was intensely personal since he had nearly died in the Honduran jungle, dumped there by an illegal order from Robert F. Kennedy. There was no greater enemy of Marcello than Robert F. Kennedy and vice versa. Furthermore, there was the strong evidence of Edward Becker's testimony that he had heard Marcello make an obvious threat against Kennedy. Also, FBI informant Eugene DeLaparra reported that mobster Ben Tregle and Marcello's son Tony had foreknowledge of the assassination. Finally, FBI informant Gene Sumner saw mobster Joe Poretto pass money to Lee Harvey Oswald in Marcello's Town and Country Restaurant. David Ferrie had worked for Marcello, and Ferrie and Oswald had been together in the Civil Air Patrol in New Orleans and also in the summer of 1963. Ten witnesses came forward on this matter, in addition to six witnesses who had seen the two together in Clinton, Louisiana, on a civil rights matter. Jack Martin worked in Guy Banister's office, and he indicated that Ferrie and Oswald knew each other and discussed the assassination before it occurred. All of these facts point to a close interrelationship between Marcello and the main players in the assassination.

Summary

Carlos Marcello was a dominant boss in the Mafia who controlled the New Orleans and Dallas areas. Robert F. Kennedy was determined to deport him by any means and illegally swept him off the streets of New Orleans onto an airplane that landed in Honduras. Marcello and his attorney were marooned in the jungles of El Salvador and Honduras, and Marcello nearly died returning to civilization. Among all of the possible conspirators involved in the John F. Kennedy assassination, no one would have had more reason to eliminate John F. Kennedy than Marcello. His associate, Ed Becker, quoted that his boss commented that one gets rid of a dog by cutting off its head, a reference to John F. Kennedy. The evidence is also clear that Lee Harvey Oswald and Jack Ruby had an association with the New Orleans don. Marcello's son also appeared to have foreknowledge of the assassination. As an example of Marcello's importance in New Orleans, the headlines in the local newspaper announcing that he had won the deportation trial were placed above that of the president's assassination. Any contract out to kill John F. Kennedy would have had Carlos Marcello's name in bold type.

11

The Role of the
Bay of Pigs Invasion

THE KENNEDY ADMINISTRATION WAS determined to get rid of Castro, and
the CIA delegated the task to Sam Giancana and his associates. Mafia
don Santos Trafficante had put the Giancana team in touch with two
Cubans for an attempted assassination. The first was Juan Orta Cordova, a private secretary of Castro and therefore in a position to poison Castro. By February 1961 six of these pills had been given to the
Giancana team, but Cordova lost contact with Castro and became
nervous. He went to a Venezuelan agency for protection and finally
fled to Mexico. The second individual was Tony Varona, a member of
the Democratic Revolutionary Rescue, an anti-Castro group that
helped to plan the Bay of Pigs invasion. Varona was supposed to find
someone to poison Castro but failed to do so. April 17, 1961, was the
date of the Bay of Pigs disaster. Fourteen hundred Cuban exiles were
involved; the result was 114 dead and about 1,200 captured. John F.
Kennedy cancelled the second air strike that was considered crucial
for the success of this operation. There were eight sorties from a base
in Nicaragua two days before the invasion, but they failed to wipe out
the small Cuban Air Force. A ninth flew to Miami, claiming to be part
of a group of Cuban defectors, hoping that the forces in Cuba might

JFK AND SAM

defect when it was known that others had given up. Unfortunately, no one was fooled by this maneuver.

Kennedy refused to allow the second bombing, afraid that his administration would be too closely linked to the invasion. Another probable reason for Kennedy's sudden refusal to permit the second bombing run was that U.N. Ambassador Adlai Stevenson had just come from the United Nations, where he had claimed that the United States had no involvement whatsoever in this Cuban affair. Later in the White House he learned that, in fact, the United States had been very much involved and felt extremely embarrassed by his earlier denial. Kennedy, therefore, decided against further involvement by the United States and refused to allow the second bombing run to take place. In a news conference on April 21, Kennedy, fearing further political embarrassment, said that there would be no more questions about Cuba but admitted that he was the responsible person in the government. Privately, however, he said that he followed the recommendations of the CIA and the Joint Chiefs of Staff, claiming that his mistake was to pay attention to them. Kennedy admitted to historian and friend Arthur Schlesinger that he probably made a mistake in keeping Allen Dulles as CIA director. Kennedy's closest aide, Ted Sorenson, said that the president felt misled by the CIA. Part of Kennedy's attitude likely arose from the fact that the Giancana group was not able to assassinate Castro just before the invasion. If Castro had been killed, the overthrow of the Communists would have been easy, but with Castro alive, there would have been a bigger struggle than was expected. Both Special Assistant for National Security Affairs McGeorge Bundy and John F. Kennedy knew how important the second air strike would be, but it was called it off, not as a military decision, but for political reasons. A second air strike would call attention to U.S. involvement in Cuba. Robert Maheu, who later coordinated the attempt of the Mafia to assassinate Castro, tried to cancel the invasion if there was no second air strike. Maheu reportedly believed Kennedy was criminally responsible for this disaster because he had the power to cancel the invasion at the last minute and failed to do so.

The account of Army Col. Fletcher Prouty in his book on the assassination of John F. Kennedy is very illuminating. He points out that on November 4, 1960, with the election set to take place in four days, the CIA sent a cable to the Bay of Pigs project office in Guatemala to proceed with training of land, sea, and airborne assault forces. This was called Operation Trinidad. Prouty was the last officer to brief the outgoing secretary of defense on the subject of Operation Trinidad on his final day in office. The final tactical plan for the Cuban invasion was approved by President Kennedy on Sunday, April 16, 1961, at 1:45 p.m. It could well have succeeded, but it was based on the use of B26s piloted by four Cuban exiles to destroy Castro's small combat air force of Soviet T33s. The first air attack before the troop invasion was to be on Saturday, April 15, and in fact took place on that date and destroyed most of the Cuban airplanes, leaving only three aircraft intact. U2 photographs taken late on Saturday, April 15, showed the three T33s parked wing tip to wing tip on a small airstrip near San Diego, Cuba. One eight-gun B26 could have wiped them out as they sat on the ground, but the CIA's operational commander chose to send four B26s when only one was needed. The plan was for a land brigade to take over the airstrip after securing the beachhead, and these B26s flown by Cuban pilots could overwhelm any force set up by Castro in the area.

The second attack was scheduled to destroy Castro's three remaining aircraft at dawn on the Monday before the brigade hit the beach. It was essential that those three aircraft be eliminated first. Kennedy understood that key element of the plan when he made the decision on Sunday to proceed with the Monday morning landing. He specifically approved the dawn air strike by the B26 bombers from Nicaragua to wipe out the last three jets.

The second phase of the plan (called Operation Zapata) assumed that tens of thousands of Cubans would rise up to join the brigade and revolt against Castro. That was the plan, but between the time of Kennedy's approval at 1:45 p.m. Sunday and the time for the release of the four B26 airplanes from the Hidden Valley Base at Puerto Cabezas in Nicaragua, the vital air strike was called off. This strike was canceled specifically by the president's Special Assistant for National Security Affairs, McGeorge Bundy, in a telephone call to Charles Cabell, deputy director of the CIA.

At 1:00 a.m. on April 17 the home phone of Col. Fletcher Prouty rang in Virginia with a call from Nicaragua. It was his old friend, the CIA commander in Nicaragua. The commander was upset and told Prouty the air strike had been delayed, claiming that anything after a 2:00 a.m. departure would destroy the whole plan, because the B26s would not be able to arrive before sunrise; the brigade was to hit the beach at dawn. All this would alert the air defenses and the T33s of Castro's Air Force, and "We will lose our targets on the ground." The caller urged Prouty to call Cabell at the Operation Zapata office and demand the immediate release of the B26s.

Prouty could hear the airplanes' engines running in the background. The commander suggested, "If I got on my bike and rode across the field, the Cubans would take off without formal orders." Both Prouty and his friend in Nicaragua wished that he had done that, but Prouty was unable to reach either Cabell or CIA Director Allen Dulles, who was out of the country.

The Bay of Pigs operation came that close to success. After that phone call, Prouty reached the CIA's Operation Zapata office and suggested that they release the B26s "on Kennedy's orders" or the whole effort would fail. The CIA's tactical commander told him that the situation was in the hands of Bundy, Cabell, and Secretary of State Dean Rusk. Everybody understood that if the B26s in Nicaragua did not leave soon, the plan would fail. Later on it was learned that someone called Nicaragua and said not to worry, that other B26s would knock out the three T33 airplanes. That did not happen. This is one reason why so many B26s were shot down later that day. The pilots believed there would be no air opposition, least of all from any T33s. The result of this canceled bombing attack was that the three T33 jets, scarcely considered any kind of real threat, shot down several brigade B26s, sank the supply ships offshore, and raked the beach with heavy gunfire. These three T33 jets alone were responsible for Castro's victory over the brigade. Kennedy's canceling of the dawn air strike created his own defeat and brought the whole burden down on the shoulders of the new president.

On April 19 the CIA's Richard Bissell was called to the White House because four American pilots of the Alabama Air National Guard ignored orders and had actually taken off for Cuba, but they were too late to be effective. Two U.S. B26s were shot down, and Robert F. Kennedy then met with Bissell and reportedly said that those American pilots "had better be dead." His only concern was his brother's image, not the pilots. Bissell told others, like Jacob Esterline of the CIA, that Robert F. Kennedy wanted those pilots dead. Bissell paid the inevitable price and was permitted to resign in early 1962.

Marcus Raskin was a disarmament expert with Bundy in the White House, and on his first day met with his staff and asked, "What has been learned about Cuba?" He was then told not to come to any more staff meetings as an example of how delicate the topic was in the White House.

Later, on April 22, 1961, President Kennedy directed Army Gen. Maxwell Taylor, Adm. Arleigh Burke, Allen Dulles, and Attorney General Robert F. Kennedy to give him a report on the immediate causes of the Operation Zapata failure in the Bay of Pigs. That elaborate report by Taylor was given to Kennedy in the form of a long letter dated June 13. Taylor reported that the blame for the defeat of the brigade came down to one telephone call, keeping in mind that President Kennedy had previously approved the dawn air strike at 1:45 p.m. on April 16, 1961. Quoting from the forty-third paragraph of the Taylor letter: "At about 9:30 p.m. on April 16 Mr. McGeorge Bundy, Special Assistant to the president, telephoned General Cabell of the CIA to inform him the dawn air strikes planned on the following morning should not be launched until they could be conducted from a strip within the beachhead."

After the Bay of Pigs fiasco, Robert F. Kennedy became the driving force for a renewed effort to depose Castro, and he became a very unpopular official in the government, especially in the CIA. The new plan was called Operation Mongoose, and it was run by Air Force Gen. Edward G. Lansdale. William Harvey was responsible for the executive action referred to as ZR/RIFLE, which involved plans for assassination; the mob therefore was working for Harvey. And Harvey believed this action was more a Kennedy family vendetta than a U.S. operation. Harvey then took over a similar task force, called Task Force W, which also involved Cuba.

Although Robert F. Kennedy denied that he and his brother had anything to do with the Cuban assassination attempt, the brothers were fully informed about the Bay of Pigs invasion. Army Gen. Maxwell Taylor criticized the CIA in his report, saying that they had not made clear enough to the president the need for the second air strike. He put the blame on the CIA and not the president.

Relationships between the CIA, the Mafia, and the Kennedys began to deteriorate. In September 1961 John F. Kennedy announced that Allen Dulles would be replaced by John A. McCone as CIA director. Walter Elder, who was an executive assistant to McCone, noticed there was intense dislike in the CIA for Robert F. Kennedy. As reported by Seymour Hersh, Thomas Parrott of the CIA intelligence group indicated that Robert F. Kennedy was an "unprincipled sinister little bastard." Samuel Halpern, the executive officer involved with Task Force W, said, "I don't know how Robert F. Kennedy squared in his own mind. On the one hand, he allegedly was going after the Mafia to destroy them; on the other hand, he was using them for information about Cuba." Of course, Robert F. Kennedy was more than going after them in 1961; it was the most sweeping campaign ever waged against gangsters.

Summary

The three Mafia operatives (Giancana, Trafficante, and Rosselli) had not been successful in killing Castro, so the CIA began to train anti-Castro Cuban refugees in the southern United States for an eventual invasion of Cuba. Two days before the landing of these Cubans, eight air sorties were successful in destroying a portion of the Castro forces, but three Cuban airplanes remained in service on the ground. The plan was to release a second attack from Nicaragua to eliminate these three aircraft, and on April 16, 1961, the day before the invasion, Kennedy approved the plan. But Adlai E. Stevenson had just strongly protested in the United Nations that the United States had nothing to do with the events in Cuba and was severely embarrassed when he later found the opposite to be true. For political reasons, Kennedy decided not to involve U.S. forces further and refused to allow the second bomber group to take off from Nicaragua to arrive at dawn before the invasion. Still, the invasion proceeded on April 17, but the three intact Cuban planes shot down many B26s, sank supply ships, killed many anti-Castro soldiers, and were very much responsible for the failure of the Bay of Pigs invasion. But rather than admit his role in the failure of the plan, the president blamed the CIA, said he would break up the organization, and fired the three major players, including Director Allen Dulles. Not only those three individuals but many others in the CIA felt that Kennedy double-crossed them in his failure to back up the Cuban invasion, resulting in the death of more than a hundred soldiers and imprisonment and torture of more than a thousand.

12

Making Enemies

Robert S. McNamara was Kennedy's secretary of defense. He had been a statistician during World War II. He did not know aircraft well, but he had his eye on a large amount of money for a tactical fighter plane, the TFX (which later became the F111). Discussions for the contract to build this fighter had been narrowed down to the Boeing Aircraft Company and a joint proposal presented by General Dynamics and the Grumman Aircraft Company. The money available was the tremendous amount (in those days) of $6.5 billion. Kennedy added Labor Secretary Arthur Goldberg, a World War II OSS (old CIA) veteran, to the TFX team, and it was Goldberg's idea that this $6.5 billion could be used with great political advantage for Kennedy throughout the country. The money could make the Democratic Party stronger for the reelection of the president. Col. Fletcher Prouty had an office a few doors down the hall from the suite of rooms where this matter was debated. There was a huge map on the walls of this suite showing in color every county that Kennedy carried in the 1960 election and every county that had gone to Nixon. All the contractors who could work on the TFX project were marked on the county maps, and Goldberg's team marked the site of each facility, taking into account how many workers it employed, how much money would be spent there, and calculating other political advantages.

McNamara managed to string out four evaluation studies, and in 1962 the Senate held hearings on which company should receive this contract. Gen. Curtis LeMay, chief of staff of the air force, told the Senate committee that more than a quarter of a million man-hours had been poured into this selection process. Everything had been made ready for a decision in favor of Boeing right after the Kennedy inauguration. But with the idea from Goldberg and McNamara that the selection should be political, the decision was pushed back for months. Every county across the nation was considered while the politicians tried to determine how they could get as much political gain as possible out of the process. On November 23, 1962, more than two years after the election, the decision was made. Secretary of the Air Force Eugene Zuckert confided to a few friends that the decision had been made in favor of Boeing. But the Goldberg theme was that the General Dynamics–Grumman proposal would get a greater return politically for the Democrats at the ballot box. Behind the scenes the totally unexpected decision had been made, and it overruled the opinion of the military. McNamara then scheduled a meeting for November 24 to announce the decision, ignoring the vote of the selection board and all the senior military members. He announced his choice for the General Dynamics–Grumman proposal.

As we mentioned in chapter 7, in August, about three months before the November 24, 1962, announcement, a break-in occurred at the apartment of Judith Campbell, one of John F. Kennedy's lovers. Author Seymour Hersh, in his book *The Dark Side of Camelot*, suggests that whatever was found there may have been used to blackmail Kennedy into making the controversial award of the TFX fighter plane. Those who had broken into Campbell's apartment were part of the security operation of General Dynamics, which was subsequently awarded the TFX contract. Hersh claims that all of this was known because the FBI spied on the spies of General Dynamics. It is also possible that the Kennedys pressured the General Dynamics group to rescue dirty little secrets in Campbell's apartment as a price to pay for the contract.

Gen. Curtis LeMay later testified that no one from the air force, including himself, had ever recommended the General Dynamics–Grumman model, and the members of the selection board who had voted for Boeing were stunned by this development. One member said, "I was surprised that the decision was made without consultation. I don't consider this the normal procedure. I thought that we had had such a clear cut and unanimous opinion all up and down the line that I was completely surprised at the decision."

Prouty stated that, from the Kennedy point of view, the TFX and other such aircraft were only devices that could be used to direct money into political districts to assure the reelection of Kennedy. The real Kennedy agenda became clear with this TFX decision and was made even clearer by the existence of the "Special Study Group" that would deal with the "possibility and desirability of peace." Awarding contracts based on the politics of reelection had a great impact on the enormous military machine of this nation. Many believed that the Kennedy plan, using the military as a political tool, jeopardized not hundreds of millions, not even billions, but possibly trillions of dollars, shaking the very foundation of American society.

President Kennedy was asked on a number of occasions in news conferences about this controversial decision to award the TFX contract to General Dynamics. In a news conference on March 21, 1963, five separate questions were asked about this decision. He was asked if he played a role in the decision. He answered that the decision rested completely with the Defense Department. Still, there was another question about the matter in a news conference on April 3, 1963, and two questions on May 8. During the latter conference, Kennedy was asked if there was any relationship between the fact that Adm. George W. Anderson was not retained as chief of navy operations and the fact that he opposed Defense Secretary McNamara on the TFX contract. Kennedy answered, "There is no relationship. The admiral will be asked to continue to serve since I have the highest confidence in him." As a follow-up the president was asked in what post the admiral would serve, and Kennedy replied that he would not say what post that would be. On August 20 another question was asked about the relationship of Secretary of the Navy Fred Korth to the TFX contract and if there would be a conflict of interest for him. Kennedy answered that he had the highest regard for Korth and the matter had been looked into for many months. Finally, in a news conference on October 31 a question was asked about the fact that Korth had worked for the Continental National Bank of Fort Worth while he was serving as secretary of the navy, and he also took part in the decision on a contract involving the bank's major customer—General Dynamics. Kennedy was asked if he thought that this fulfilled the requirements of the code of ethics in the government. The president's answer was that he had no evidence that Korth benefited improperly during his term of office. On the next day, November 1, 1963, Korth was no longer secretary of the navy. Thus, the press was aware of the many questionable interrelationships in this TFX contract.

Other events helped to shape Kennedy's relationship with the military-industrial complex. On April 17, 1961, the Cuban brigade was defeated in Cuba, and three days later President Kennedy, who was obviously upset over the disaster in Cuba, dealt with another troubled area and accepted a plan called the Counter Insurgency Program for Vietnam. He directed Deputy Secretary of Defense Roswell Gilpatric to make recommendations on how to prevent the Communist takeover of Vietnam. On April 20, 1961, Kennedy began to understand how the CIA and the Defense Department operated in the amazing world of underhanded secret operations. It was also the day that CIA Director Allen Dulles's influence on the Kennedy administration began to decline.

The CIA was to take another hit. Two months later, on June 28, 1961, Kennedy issued National Security Action Memorandum (NSAM) No. 55, which essentially made the Joint Chiefs of Staff responsible for the cold war, effectively downgrading and removing the CIA from cold-war operations. Cold-war operations were defined in this memo and were described as clandestine operations sponsored by the highest authority of the U.S. government in support of an existing government friendly to the United States or a rebel group seeking to overthrow a government hostile to the United States. In the memo, President Kennedy made clear his relationship with the Joint Chiefs of Staff and stated, "I regard the Joint Chiefs of Staff as my principal military advisers responsible both for initiating advice to me and for responding to requests for advice. I expect their advice to come to me direct and unfiltered." This memo was very different from the previous policy that Allen Dulles had perfected over the past decade. In this case, policy statements went from the National Security Council directly to the CIA for all clandestine operations. In the past, the Joint Chiefs had not usually participated in the overall operational planning with the CIA, but they were involved whenever CIA operators approached them for support from the army, air force, and navy.

Following NSAM No. 55 was NSAM No. 56, which dealt with the evaluation of paramilitary requirements, which then led to NSAM No. 57, on the responsibility for paramilitary operations. This latter memo indicated, "Where such a clandestine operation is to be wholly covert or disavowable it may be assigned to the CIA provided that it is within the normal capability of the agency." But when a large paramilitary operation required a significant number of trained military personnel, primary responsibility would go to the Department of Defense with the CIA in a supporting role. All of the latter memos limited the CIA, mainly to its lawful responsibility: coordination of intelligence.

On July 11, 1961, the CIA took another hit when Kennedy announced the establishment of the Defense Intelligence Agency (DIA). Obviously this organization had overlapping responsibilities with what the CIA had done in the past. During discussions of what went wrong in Cuba, both John F. Kennedy and Robert F. Kennedy determined that Allen Dulles and other top-level CIA staffers had to go. Dulles left on November 29, 1961.

In the latter part of May 1961 the main players of the CIA were fading fast; Gen. Maxwell Taylor became the man of the hour in the eyes of the Kennedy brothers. Taylor had been in retirement since the Eisenhower administration, but he was called out of retirement by the Kennedys. One other document played a major role in the forces that combined to bring about the assassination of President Kennedy. It was the result of meetings between Secretary of Defense McNamara, General Taylor, and President Diem of South Vietnam in Saigon at the end of September 1963. Between August and November 1963 the Kennedy administration had discussions on the Vietnam situation in at least 383 meetings and conferences. An important meeting was held on October 2, 1963, in Honolulu, Hawaii, and members of that committee dealing with the Vietnam situation were given a document to study during their nine-hour flight back to Washington. The study was compiled and written in the Joint Chiefs of Staff offices of Gen. Victor H. Krulak.

This document resulted in the NSAM No. 263, issued on October 11, 1963, by Secretary of Defense McNamara and General Taylor. The memo included the information, "No formal announcement [will] be made of the implementation of plans to withdraw the 1,000 U.S. military personnel by the end of 1963." Although this document was not declassified until July 6, 1976, it was immediately known by various groups. Kennedy's intention to withdraw the troops was clear, but he also intended to keep this plan somewhat secret so there would be no formal announcement.

In association with NSAM No. 263, but as a separate document, President Kennedy directed the following guidance to be issued to all concerned: "The central object of the United States in Vietnam was to assist the people and the government of that country to win their contest against North Vietnam. The objectives of the United States were to withdraw personnel. The provisional government of South Vietnam should be assisted by the United States. The United States should avoid either the appearance or the reality of public recrimination from one part of it against another." This memo was written by McGeorge Bundy, special assistant to the president for national security affairs. The important question is what type of recrimination Bundy expected. This memo was written on the day before Kennedy was killed, and one question is whether or not Bundy had anticipated the assassination, and did he believe that there would be some enormous uprising in the United States as a result of the assassination.

The other interesting point is that the official U.S. Armed Forces newspaper, called *Pacific Stars and Stripes,* published on October 4, 1963, had the headline: WHITE HOUSE REPORT: U.S. TROOPS SEEN OUT OF VIETNAM BY '65. The *New York Times* also carried the story on November 21, 1963. But the strange feature of this matter is that there are so many newsmen and historians who have claimed that the NSAM No. 263 never existed. Prouty was in the Pentagon at that time and believed that the members of the "power elite" of the military-industrial complex and their powerful bankers believed they had already been seriously damaged by Kennedy's plans and policies by the middle of 1963. NSAM No. 263 was an enormous threat to them, and President Kennedy seemed certain to be reelected to a second term. Thus they realized that Kennedy had to be stopped before his 1964 election campaign. NSAM No. 263 further concluded that the U.S. military campaign had made great progress and continued to progress in Vietnam, and that a program should be established to train Vietnamese, who could then train their countrymen. This training had been performed up to that time by U.S. personnel. Also, the Defense Department should be prepared to withdraw one thousand U.S. military personnel by the end of 1964, and that complete withdrawal should be accomplished by the end of 1965. Three days after John F. Kennedy's assassination the Pentagon reevaluated its position, claiming that it could not withdraw troops. Later, NSAM No. 273 appeared on November 26, 1963. In many ways this was the antithesis of NSAM No. 263. It was drafted by President Kennedy on November 21, 1963, but not authenticated until signed by Bundy after President Johnson was in office. This memo seemed more to deal with potential emergency situations for the United States than any particular connection to the administration's Vietnam policy as described by NSAM No. 263.

Removal of U.S. troops from Vietnam on the basis of NSAM No. 263 would have had a great impact on the military-industrial complex that provided weaponry for the war in Vietnam. If anything moves people to action, it is money, especially lots of money. NSAM No. 263 would have had a huge impact on the suppliers of the war machine that now viewed Kennedy as their enemy. There are a number of such factors in evidence just before Kennedy's assassination, and these factors can be considered circumstantial evidence. But Colonel Prouty reminds us that over 120 years ago Judge Advocate Juan Bigham observed, "A conspiracy is rarely if ever proved by a positive testimony. Unless one of the original conspirators betrays his companions and gives evidence against them, their guilt can be proved only by circumstantial evidence. It is said by some writers on evidence that such circumstances are stronger than positive proof. A witness swearing positively may misrepresent or swear falsely, but the circumstances cannot lie." Thus Colonel Prouty believes that Kennedy's NSAM No. 263 likely created new enemies against the president, namely the suppliers of the war machine.

Prouty further believes that it is very strange that the president's entire cabinet was on an airplane on the way to Hawaii at the time of the assassination. The absence of the cabinet while the president was out of Washington seemed very strange indeed. In addition, at that same time Prouty had been selected to be the military escort officer for a group of VIP civilian guests to a naval station in Antarctica. Prouty has always wondered whether that strange invitation to Antarctica, removing him so far from Washington DC, as if to get him out of the loop, might have been connected to the assassination. It is a fact that Prouty's removal to Antarctica was directed by an arm of the government. But was it a coincidence?

Summary

The enormous budget of $6.5 billion to develop the TFX jet fighter was to go to the Boeing Company, and after a quarter of a million man-hours of study, Gen. Curtis LeMay said that all representatives from the air force were in favor of Boeing rather than the competition, the

General Dynamics–Grumman consortium. Secretary of the Air Force Eugene Zuckert also indicated that the decision was clearly for Boeing. But Labor Secretary Arthur Goldberg had been developing a map of the United States near Fletcher Prouty's office in the Pentagon with each county designated according to its number of votes in the 1960 election. Goldberg and Kennedy had decided that it would be a political advantage to give the contract to General Dynamics–Grumman and better secure Kennedy's reelection in 1964. Thus the contract was so awarded, which stunned Congress and the air force. This decision also had a tremendous impact on the military. National Security Action Memo (NSAM) No. 55 impacted the CIA, removing it from cold-war operations and giving this function to the Joint Chiefs of Staff, further diminishing the importance of the CIA. NSAM No. 263 created a new set of enemies—suppliers of the war machine—for Kennedy. This latter memo indicated that all U.S. troops would be pulled out of Vietnam by the end of 1965. Thus the enemies against Kennedy created in these actions included the air force, Boeing, the CIA, and especially the military-industrial complex.

13

The Role of
the FBI

THE STRONGEST, ALTHOUGH STILL indirect, evidence that the FBI was a
player in the Kennedy assassination comes in a well-documented vol-
ume by Mark North entitled *Act of Treason: The Role of J. Edgar Hoover
in the Assassination of President Kennedy.* This book was published in
1991 and includes a great amount of material obtained through the
Freedom of Information Act. The value of North's book is the revela-
tion of illegal and questionable activities carried on by the FBI under
J. Edgar Hoover's guidance. The illegal information came from electronic bugs called ELSUR, an abbreviation for Electronic Surveillance.
The other illegal program was called COINTELPRO, an abbreviation
for Counterintelligence Programs. Both programs were set up by
Hoover and were hidden from the rank-and-file FBI investigators. Information from these illegal wiretaps and break-ins was sent directly
to a special file room. Only Hoover and a few top aides had access to
this material. It was brought in by a system called AIRTEL, an abbreviation for Airborne Telecommunications. Hoover's office was called
SOG, which stood for Seat of Government.

Files kept in this special file room were not part of the central
records of the FBI. The only persons allowed to see this material be-
sides Hoover were Associate Director Clyde Tolson and Organized

Crime Division Chief Courtney Evans. This secret material included transcripts of illegal wiretaps of key Mafia figures across the country. In the COINTELPRO program, FBI agents conducted illegal break-ins to get special information. North's book includes samples of this information on the Mafia on nearly a day-by-day basis from November 6, 1960, to May 8, 1964. We will give you the important events in chronological order throughout the crucial times of the early 1960s.

The main thesis is that Hoover was aware of the Marcello contract on John F. Kennedy from a very early time. Hoover's motive for hiding this vital information from the Secret Service was to aid and abet the contract against the president. A successful hit on Kennedy would allow Hoover to stay on as director of the FBI past his seventieth birthday. And certain events lay the groundwork for Hoover's involvement, but they also involve Lyndon B. Johnson. For example, on Saturday, June 3, 1961, there was a report that U.S. Agriculture Department employee Henry Marshall was found murdered, shot five times with his own bolt-action rifle. We don't know the details of what Hoover found in his investigation of this death, but it is significant that it never went further than this preliminary investigation. It is especially interesting since Henry Marshall was a key figure in the Billie Sol Estes criminal investigation. The close relationship between Estes and Johnson was a very important factor that could have damaged any hopes of Johnson's continuing as the vice presidential candidate on the Kennedy ticket in the upcoming election. Protecting Johnson's position as future presidential material was also a motive of Hoover, who was very friendly with the vice president.

On Saturday, December 9, 1961, the FBI ELSUR records show that Sam Giancana and Johnny Rosselli were recorded. These records show that Giancana had secretly made large campaign contributions for Kennedy's election, and these monies were funneled through Joseph P. Kennedy. From these tapes Hoover first realized that Giancana had given Kennedy financial backing and also had arranged that the Cook County vote in Chicago would be so overwhelming as to allow Kennedy to win the election. Three days later there was another tape of Giancana and Rosselli. In this conversation Giancana was very upset with Frank Sinatra for not being able to convince the president about certain matters, and Robert F. Kennedy was also discussed. Hoover then contacted Attorney General Kennedy, his immediate supervisor, to tell him that he knew Giancana had contacted Joseph Kennedy at least three times in recent months. These tapes show that there was a great deal of communication between Giancana and Joseph P. Kennedy about the president.

On December 14, 1961, Hoover sent a memo to Robert F. Kennedy about Giancana's secret campaign donations to John F. Kennedy through Joseph P. Kennedy. On the next day, Vice President Johnson arranged for a private dinner with Hoover to discuss how to contain the Billie Sol Estes investigation. This investigation involved a huge swindle of the federal government by getting government payments for nonexistent cotton crops in Texas and other imaginary crops that were never planted. Two weeks later it was clear to the investigators of the Estes case that another of Johnson's major activities was the wheeling and dealing of the aerospace industry as well as vending-machine deals involving Bobby Baker and lobbyist Fred Black. These deals later became a scandal for Johnson.

In January 1961, attempting to deny the existence of the Mafia, Hoover stated, "No single individual or coalition of racketeers dominates organized crime across the nation." At this same time Robert F. Kennedy's war against the Mafia was beginning to make progress on many fronts. In January 1962 another ELSUR tape of Giancana came to Hoover's attention. Giancana was discussing the pending Cook County Sheriff's election with Chicago politician John D'Arco. One candidate was former FBI agent Roswell Spencer.

Giancana said, "Spencer is like Kennedy. He'll get what he wants out of you but you won't get anything out of him." This shows Giancana's early frustration that he did not get what he thought he was going to get from the Kennedys after the election. An AIRTEL recording was sent to Hoover in January 1962 in which Giancana commented, "That's right. Well, they got the whip and they're in office and that's it, so they are gonna knock us guys out of the box and make us defenseless." He was referring to Robert F. Kennedy's war against the Mafia, but we should keep in mind that Giancana may not necessarily have been as much damaged by this war as others were, specifically Carlos Marcello.

Giancana's sudden rise to power in the Mafia was in part because of the prison terms of the bosses above him. Had they not gone to prison, he might not have risen to his position as early as he did. The Mafia groups who suffered most from Robert F. Kennedy's war were the Southern families of Marcello and Trafficante and to a lesser extent the Eastern families in Philadelphia and New York. An example of the effect of the war on the Mafia can be seen in this Washington DC press report of February 2, 1962: "The manicured mobsters who rule Chicago's rackets have departed for Miami, en masse; crime czars from other cities are also converging on Miami. The best guess is that they are heading south to discuss what to do about Attorney General Robert F. Kennedy. Using his influence with the White House, he has united the feuding federal enforcement agencies into the most formidable army a lawman could ever combine to wage war upon organized crime. They now keep all the nation's top racketeers under constant scrutiny."

On Thursday, March 22, 1962, the famous confrontation took place between Hoover and John F. Kennedy over Judith Campbell. In a private luncheon Hoover confronted the president with his documented information that Campbell had visited the president on several occasions. After Hoover left, Kennedy said to Kenneth O'Donnell, his aide, "Get rid of that bastard. He is the biggest bore." Later Kennedy made his last call to Campbell. The attempt of Hoover to blackmail the president had many effects. Probably the most important affected Joseph P. Kennedy, whose crippling stroke may well have been brought on by this event.

Hoover's attempt at blackmail had failed, both with regard to Giancana's illegal contributions to Kennedy's campaign and the liaisons with Judith Campbell and others. The reason the blackmail plan failed was that the Kennedys had comparable blackmail on Hoover regarding his homosexual escapades and his own Mafia connections.

John F. Kennedy began to distance himself from Frank Sinatra on March 23, 1962. On a trip to the West Coast to give a speech, the president had planned to stay with Frank Sinatra in Palm Springs. But at the last minute he canceled, not the trip, but this visit to Sinatra, and instead opted to stay with Bing Crosby in the same area. Sinatra was so offended by this snubbing that he broke off his relationship with Kennedy in-law Peter Lawford. It seems likely that Robert F. Kennedy was behind this sudden change in John F. Kennedy's plans, because on the next day the president attended a dinner party at Sinatra's home where Marilyn Monroe was present.

On the same day, at the Bowie Racetrack, in Maryland, Vice President Johnson and Hoover met to discuss the crisis in the Billie Sol Estes case that threatened to break open the connection between Estes and Johnson.

On April 4, 1962, the decomposed body of George Krutilek was found in the sandhills near Clint, Texas. Krutilek was slumped in his car with a hose from the exhaust pipe stuck in the window. But the El Paso County pathologist concluded that Krutilek did not die from the carbon monoxide, and an El Paso television station claimed he was murdered. Krutilek was the accountant who had all of the information about Billie Sol Estes's scams and had documents that would convict Estes. Thus two mysterious murders—Henry Marshall's and George Krutilek's—both in Texas and connected with the Billie Sol Estes story, with huge government scams, implicated the vice president. In the months of April and May 1962, Congressman Bill Kramer (R-FL) was preparing impeachment proceedings against Johnson because of his association with Estes and the illegal grain storage and nonexistent cotton crop operations in Texas. Johnson repeatedly denounced the "false allegations" that linked him with Estes's financial dealings. To conceal Johnson's involvement, Hoover and Cartha DeLoach, who was in charge of the FBI Crime Records division, and lobbyist Thomas Corcoran managed to downplay Johnson's role. But in order to force some closure in August 1962, Johnson associate Morris Jaffe purchased the bankrupt Estes estate in Texas for $7 million. Later that year the prosecution of Estes began, concluding the next year on March 28 with his conviction on mail-fraud charges that involved $24 million.

Was there also a Mafia connection in this Johnson-Estes scandal? The most likely candidate for this would, of course, be Carlos Marcello, who was in charge of the New Orleans and Texas Mafia. But the connection was actually with Teamsters boss Jimmy Hoffa. The linking of Estes and Hoffa became evident from tapes on May 16, 1962, that showed a $12 million loan granted by Hoffa's Teamsters Union to Estes. Nine days later the *Chicago Tribune* reported that Estes had threatened to "go to the top" to get his loan, and this likely was a reference to the vice president. In June 1962 informant Edward Partin, a Teamsters Union official, spoke to Federal officials of Hoffa's plan to assassinate Robert F. Kennedy. Later Hoffa was talked out of this plan, but he eventually played a key role in promoting the final Mafia contract against John F. Kennedy.

In August and September 1962, Hoover became acutely aware through his illegal wiretaps that Marcello had put out a contract on John F. Kennedy. The reasons for Marcello's decision range from the fact that he was under federal indictment, that he faced the threat of deportation, that he had nearly lost his life in the San Salvadoran and Honduran jungles from Robert F. Kennedy's illegal kidnapping, and that his gambling associate, Sam Saia, had not been appointed to the Appeals Board of the Immigration and Naturalization Service as a way of avoiding deportation. Also, Marcello's gambling network was being forced into court by Robert F. Kennedy, and this network included key figures linked to Hoffa and Santos Trafficante. Furthermore, Robert F. Kennedy was calling for laws to waive the Fifth Amendment protection by compelling members of the Mafia to testify if they were granted immunity. This key legislation would eliminate the Fifth Amendment as a way to avoid testifying against fellow Mafia figures. The corrupt director of the Bureau of Narcotics and a close friend of Hoover, Harry Anslinger, had also just been replaced by a man handpicked by John F. Kennedy.

As a part of the story of Marcello's contract on the president, Jack Ruby discussed the details of the contract with Marcello's lieutenants. He made many calls to mobster Louis McWillie, who operated out of the Thunderbird Hotel in Las Vegas. Also at the same hotel was Clifford Jones, who was associated with Johnson's aide Bobby Baker. These relationships show possible links between the underworld and the Federal Government. Ruby's debt to the Internal Revenue Service was more than forty thousand dollars, and his need for cash kept him interested in the Marcello contract.

Through all of these illegal wiretaps and his interest in pornographic pictures obtained secretly on politicians, Hoover's character comes into focus. He was an active homosexual with partner Clyde Tolson, the number-two man in the FBI. They were inseparable throughout their careers. But in Hoover we see a man whose interest in pornography was obsessive. He gambled on a daily basis, especially at racetracks, where he would use an associate to place his bets on races secretly fixed by the Mafia. He was a fairly heavy drinker, usually allowing others to pay for his drinks, both at dinners during a regular workweek and during vacation. He spoke frequently about morality at Boy Scout meetings and at political groups, constantly reminding the public that immorality leads to Communism. But the difference between his public self and his private life was alarming.

Hoover's double standard, holding others to the highest of moral measures and yet allowing himself to indulge all his own desires, derives from a complex psychological makeup. In the early 1960s Hoover had absolute power over the FBI and controlled every detail, including the agents' dress and manner, their deportment, and their private lives. Nevertheless, he was a friend of the Mafia, particularly through his contacts with Frank Costello and Meyer Lansky of the New York families. This relationship was firmed up after Lansky obtained photographs of Hoover's homosexual (and possibly pedophilic) activity. Lansky blackmailed Hoover into protecting his drug racketeering. Bob McDonnell, Giancana's lawyer and Antoinette's husband, confirms that the Mafia had a great deal of evidence of Hoover's homosexual and cross-dressing activities. Hoover's anti-liberal, anti-black, and anti-Semitic attitudes permeated the FBI and were transmitted to the lowest-level workers in the agency. In the late 1950s and early 1960s, Hoover directed the FBI to go after the American Communist Party, infiltrating the party to the degree that FBI double agents comprised almost a third of the party membership. This foolishness was exposed by John F. Kennedy and Robert F. Kennedy in many speeches and editorials, not by naming Hoover directly, but by making reference to the stupidity of his policies. Of course, Robert F. Kennedy's war against the Mafia was, in part, Joseph P. Kennedy's idea to get rid of the obligations the Kennedy family owed the Italian Mafia as well as an attack on protected narcotics racketeering left untouched by Hoover.

The battle between the Irish Kennedys and the Italian Mafia can be placed into historical perspective. The Irish had emigrated to the United States in large numbers in the first half of the nineteenth century, before the Italian immigration of the late nineteenth and early twentieth centuries. As a result, the Irish were firmly entrenched in city government, with both mayors and city police dominated by Irish in most large industrial cities. The Italians had little chance of taking over these civilian groups and did not have control over legislatures or political organizations. As a result, the Italians formed a paralegal organization modeled after the Sicilian Mafia organization of the late eighteenth and early nineteenth centuries. Thus, to Mafia insiders, the Marcello contract against Kennedy looked like a typical mob contract against an Irish gang leader.

In April 1963 Bobby Baker purchased a home in Spring Valley near Washington DC, close to both his friend Fred Black and his long-term mentor, Lyndon Johnson. Black belonged to the exclusive Quorum Club run by Baker in Washington DC, a high-class prostitution network used to lure congressmen and government bureaucrats into sexual activity. In some cases they were taped and blackmailed. In

May 1963 Baker made a special trip to California to try to convince Governor Edmund G. "Pat" Brown to end competitive bidding for a lease on the Del Mar Racetrack. Baker prevailed and no bidding occurred. This track was one of the tracks where the Mafia fixed races on which Hoover often placed bets (and won). This is also the track that Texas millionaire Clint Murchison Sr. had acquired without competitive bidding, partially to favor Hoover who made his annual vacation to that part of California.

On May 10, 1963, in a stunning setback for Attorney General Robert F. Kennedy, all defendants in a Marcello gambling case were found not guilty by a New Orleans jury, with at least one of the jurors bribed at the trial. It was seventeen days later that wiretaps showed the Mafia families in the Northeast were furious with the Kennedys, and the next month a number of racketeers, particularly from Chicago, met in Dallas for a series of meetings at Jack Ruby's Carousel Club. These meetings were supposedly about prostitution and gambling, but likely involved the original planning around the Marcello contract to kill Kennedy. The timing was about six months before the actual assassination. This was also consistent with the claim of shooter Deadeye, who said that six months before the assassination a decision was made to volunteer Chuckie Nicoletti's team as Chicago's contribution to the shooters used in the assassination.

At the least, Hoover appears to be an accomplice in the Marcello contract, because he did not inform the Secret Service of its existence and took steps to expose it. Hiding the activities of the Mafia marks Hoover as a conspirator, because his primary duty was to warn the president of this potential danger. In addition, all physical evidence from the assassination was shipped to Hoover with orders that no one was to reveal any information. He was in a commanding position with regard to all the physical evidence and FBI testimony.

On June 6, 1963, tapes indicated that the Eastern Mafia families wondered exactly what action they should take against John F. Kennedy. On one of these tapes, Mafia chief Stephano Magaddino of Buffalo said, "Here we are situated with this administration. We got all the way from the president down against us. But we got to resist. Today. You see this table? [Hits table] You have got to do something material." On the same day Jack Ruby's attorney, Graham Koch, told the IRS he would settle the tax delinquency account for a total of $39,129. His ability to settle this account likely was related to the fact that Ruby would be obtaining a similar sum of money in the near future—around the time of the assassination.

A final public break between Robert F. Kennedy and Lyndon B. Johnson occurred on June 18, 1963, when there was a sharp public exchange between them, to the effect that the vice president was made to look like a fraud. From this point on they avoided each other. Johnson undoubtedly blamed Robert F. Kennedy for pushing the Estes case and also a case against aide Bobby Baker. Both cases could have led either to an impeachment of Johnson or at least serious legal problems.

In August 1963 Jack Ruby visited Chicago and contacted mobster Lenny Patrick, who in February had put out a contract on Benjamin Lewis, an associate of Chicago Mayor Richard J. Daley. The main issues for Ruby were supposedly labor disputes, and he was working through Chicago mobster Dave Yaras. It is also important to know that Patrick was not only part of the Chicago mob but also had close relationships to Marcello and Trafficante and was their contact with Yaras in Chicago. Thus there were close ties between Ruby and the Chicago, New Orleans, and Florida mobs.

Summary

This chapter shows how J. Edgar Hoover learned through illegal tapes a great deal about the Mafia and their plans to assassinate President Kennedy in the early 1960s. His major motivation in not sharing the information with the Secret Service was his desire to stay on as director of the FBI beyond the usual retirement age, and the Kennedys stood in his way. Hoover and the Kennedys became great enemies, especially after Hoover let John F. Kennedy know that he knew about one of Kennedy's girlfriends, Judith Campbell. Hoover was also very much aware of Sam Giancana and his relationship to Johnny Rosselli and Frank Sinatra. The plan to kill the president was often referred to as the Marcello contract, and Hoover was aware of it and of the relationship between Carlos Marcello, Jimmy Hoffa, and Billie Sol Estes. Estes was involved with Vice President Lyndon B. Johnson, and the murders of George Krutilek and Henry Marshall were associated with the Estes case. Johnson was further implicated in several scandals because aide Bobby Baker ran the Quorum Club, which was used to blackmail congressmen and government bureaucrats. Hoover's contacts with the Mafia were especially clear in his track betting on races fixed by the mob with information relayed to the director. The major point of this chronological account of the early 1960s is that J. Edgar Hoover knew enough about the assassination but contributed to its success by not revealing the information to the Secret Service.

14

Debunking
Lee Harvey Oswald

THE SO-CALLED LONE GUNMAN theory is that Lee Harvey Oswald, and only he, was the crazed individual solely responsible for the assassination of John F. Kennedy. In the following paragraphs we will give you several reasons that argue strongly against this theory. We will also show how Oswald was involved with other individuals who were involved in the assassination. This chapter will describe the critical events of Oswald's life and how they relate to President Kennedy's assassination.

After Oswald's birth, his mother's sister, Lillian, and her husband, Charles "Dutz" Murret, became a substitute family for Oswald. Dutz was a New Orleans bookmaker who worked for Carlos Marcello. In New Orleans in the summer of 1955, between his ninth and tenth grades, Oswald was invited to weekly meetings of the student aviation organization of the Civil Air Patrol at the Lakefront Airport. His commander was Capt. David William Ferrie, who was raised a devout Catholic, attended St. Mary's Seminary in Cleveland, prepared to enter the priesthood, but left and attended Baldwin-Wallace College in Berea, Ohio. Ferrie received his pilot's license in 1944. He moved to New Orleans where he eventually worked for Marcello; in the early 1950s Ferrie worked for Eastern Airlines. At least three witnesses have confirmed that Oswald and Ferrie worked together, particularly in the Civil Air Patrol, and pictures can be seen of the two men in the same photo. Thus, these latter points demonstrate that Oswald had early connections to the Mafia through Uncle Dutz and David Ferrie.

If one were to assume that Oswald was the individual who shot Kennedy, one must consider his skills with a rifle. He was a poor shot while he was in the marines, scoring first a 212 at distances between two hundred and five hundred yards, qualifying him as a sharp-shooter, but later barely qualifying with a score of 191 as a marksman. Could he have fired the shots that struck the president under the diffi-cult circumstances of that fateful November day?

Oswald's mother, Marguerite, believed that he was an undercover agent for the U.S. government and considered his time in the Soviet Union as a cover for him. She repeated this point many times before her death from cancer in January 1982. Oswald's wife, Marina, also has always maintained his innocence. If Oswald had not been in-volved with the U.S. government, is it likely that the State Department would lend him or anyone else $435.71 to return to the United States from the Soviet Union? This sum was apparently repaid by one of the U.S. intelligence agencies, but likely not by Oswald.

Oswald was a friend of George Sergei DeMohrenschildt, a white Russian geologist involved with the CIA, especially in Guatemala dur-ing the training for the Bay of Pigs invasion. The geologist had also worked for Dallas oil billionaire Clint Murchison and had close con-tacts with the Mafia. DeMohrenschildt said that the CIA wanted him to maintain contact with Oswald, and it seems more than coincidental that this CIA geologist committed suicide on the day before he was to be interviewed about the Kennedy assassination. This contact places Oswald into a relationship with both the mob and the CIA.

On January 27, 1963, Oswald had purchased a Smith & Wesson .38 revolver for $29.95. Six weeks later, on March 12, he ordered a Mannlicher-Carcano rifle for $19.95 from Klein Sporting Goods Store in Chicago using the name A. Hidell, a fictitious name, rhyming with Fidel, his hero. This same name was forged on Selective Service cards that had his picture. This cheap rifle could hardly be used for the accurate shots required to kill Kennedy.

The pamphlets that Oswald distributed on the streets of New Orleans for Fair Play for Cuba had the 544 Camp Street address on it, which was the Newman Building, which also housed the detective agency of Guy Banister, who was closely involved with CIA and FBI activities. Across the street were offices for the Secret Service, the Office of Naval Intelligence, and other governmental organizations. Banister had been a former FBI agent in charge in Chicago, but in New Orleans he worked with David Ferrie. Delphine Roberts was Banister's private secretary, and she confirmed that Oswald did work for Banister in the summer of 1963. She indicated that Banister told her that Oswald was "working with us." This evidence ties Oswald to Banister and thus to the CIA and FBI.

Oswald was jailed on August 9, 1963, for disturbing the peace because of a fight with a Carlos Bringuier regarding the Fair Play for Cuba campaign, but he was bailed out by Emile Bruneau, an associate of Carlos Marcello and Charles "Dutz" Murret. While in jail Oswald had asked to see FBI agent John Lester Quigley, who did see him, even though it was unusual for an FBI agent to visit anyone with that kind of minor charge unless the prisoner was special in some other way. In the late summer of 1963, Oswald, Ferrie, and Clay Shaw (who was the focus of attention in New Orleans District Attorney Jim Garrison's trial on the conspiracy to kill Kennedy) took a trip to Clinton, Louisiana, for a voter rights campaign. Oswald was the only white person to register for voting at that time, and witnesses identified all three when they were seen together.

Another significant event in Oswald's life story involved Silvia Odio and her sister, Annie, whose father was in prison for attempting to assassinate Castro. On September 25, 1963, the sisters were visited by three individuals, one calling himself Leon Oswald. These men said that they were friends of Odio's father from an anti-Castro background. One called the next day and told Silvia that Leon was going to assassinate Kennedy. This event strongly suggests that this was a deliberate act to connect Oswald to the assassination before the actual murder.

Oswald supposedly visited Mexico City between September 26 and October 3, 1963, and went to the Cuban embassy, but there are many questions about this visit. Pictures that presumably show him in Mexico City have been discredited, and the description by Cuban Consul Eusebio Azcue does not fit the description of Oswald. This Mexican trip brings up the possibility of an Oswald impostor.

The proceedings of the executive session of the Warren Commission on January 27, 1964, include on page 129 the comment that Oswald worked as an informant for the FBI at two hundred dollars a month, especially around September 1962. Other questions about Oswald include the two well-known photos of him posing with a rifle, which strongly suggest, if the photos are fakes, they were a setup for Oswald as a patsy long before the assassination. The photographs are viewed by many as fakes, particularly because Oswald's wife, Marina, indicated that when she took the pictures she was actually standing in the same place where Oswald appears in the photo. Other questions involve a letter written by Oswald on November 8, 1963 to "Mr. Hunt." It reads, "I would like information concerning my position. I am asking only for information. I am suggesting that we discuss the matter fully before any steps are taken by me or anyone else." Who is this Hunt? Is it E. Howard Hunt of the CIA or H. L. Hunt, the Dallas oil man? This letter was obtained by Craig I. Zirbel, an attorney who wrote *The Texas Connection,* a book that implicates Johnson in the assassination of John F. Kennedy.

FBI agent James Hosty received a note from Oswald demanding that he stop bothering his wife, Marina. But after Oswald's death, the special agent in charge told Hosty to get rid of this note; Hosty tore it up and flushed it down a toilet. Why was it so important to get rid of the note unless there was some embarrassing relationship?

On the morning of the assassination, Oswald carried curtain rods with him to work, and he was seen by fellow worker Buell Frazier and his sister. Both of them said that the contents were too short (about two feet) to be a rifle, even if the rifle had been disassembled (more than three feet).

A major problem in Oswald's direct involvement occurred at the time of the assassination. Oswald was seen eating his lunch on the first floor with fellow worker James Jarman, and then he went to the second floor to buy a Coke and was seen by co-worker Carolyn Arnold at 12:15 p.m. while he was waiting for a phone call. The expected time of the motorcade was at 12:25 p.m., and Oswald was then four floors away from the sixth floor of the depository and the length of the building away from the sniper's nest. It is very unlikely that a possible assassin would take a chance that he could not get into position on time. Also, Dallas Police Officer Marrion L. Baker and the boss of the book depository, Roy Truly, saw Oswald on the second floor seventy to ninety seconds after the first shot had been fired at Kennedy. The time of one to one and a half minutes would not be sufficient for Oswald to move from the sniper's nest to the second floor. If there was a single assassin on the sixth floor, the perfect unobstructed shot would be on Houston Street as the motorcade approached the shooter, not on Elm Street with sunlight in the shooter's eyes and many tree branches that could block the view. On the other hand, if there were more than two shooters, there would have been a cross-fire from other locations.

The number of shots that can be identified in the assassination also indicates that there cannot be a single shooter. There were almost certainly four shots that hit John F. Kennedy; the first one was in the front of his neck at the level of the larynx, described by Dallas surgeon Dr. Robert McClelland as an entrance wound, probably from a gunman hiding under the manhole cover at the bottom of the grassy knoll (described for Central TV Enterprises in 1992). The second shot went into his back six inches below the shoulder line, just to the right of the spinal cord, and near the T2-T3 (thoracic) cord level, not at all in line with the shot in the neck. The third entered the back of his head. Both the second and third likely came from the book depository or Dal-Tex Building. The fourth hit the right temple from the direction of the grassy knoll from Deadeye's Fireball weapon. There were likely two shots coming from behind, which struck Governor Connally. One was into the right armpit, and the second involved the right wrist, ending in the left thigh. A couple of shots missed their target. One made a minor wound on bystander James Tague and left a hole in the curb, which was dug up, modified, and the spectrographic plates of the evidence were discarded. The second shot went inside the frame of the front windshield of the limousine; two others seemed to have struck different areas of the ground. This large number of shots (six to ten) could never have been fired from a single rifle with a bolt action over a maximum time of seven to eight seconds. In addition, as evidence that there was more than one shooter, many witnesses claimed they were chasing a possible assassin up the grassy knoll after the final shot had been fired. The Warren Commission recognized only three shots, including a single pristine bullet that went through the back of Kennedy, his neck, and caused all of Connally's wounds.

Another important point is that Lee Harvey Oswald had no obvious motive for this assassination. If he wanted a place in history, then why did he deny that he had killed anyone, and there were at least twelve witnesses who told the Warren Commission that Oswald had admired Kennedy. After the final shot, newsman Robert McNeil went to the knoll and then to the depository, where he saw Oswald and asked about a telephone. This was five to ten minutes after the shooting. Oswald was not racing out of the building but spoke to supervisor Bill Shelley at that time.

Many parts of the following story do not fit Oswald as the lone gunman. In the sniper nest on the sixth floor many boxes were piled up, but only a single palm print could be found on all of those boxes. Oswald worked there, so his palm prints would be expected to be found on the boxes. Furthermore, the scope of the rifle supposedly used by Oswald was so misaligned that the FBI had to put three shims under the scope to even test-fire it. It is interesting that Deputy Sheriff Eugene Boone described the rifle as a 7.65 mm Mauser and not a 6.5

mm Mannlicher-Carcano; he also said that this rifle was "worn and rusty." It was discovered as long as thirty minutes after the shooting.

It is unlikely that Dallas policeman J. D. Tippit was killed by Lee Harvey Oswald since he had a .38 revolver and Tippit was killed by bullets from an automatic pistol. Shells found at that killing did not fit Oswald's gun, and witnesses did not identify him at first but changed their minds later. The time of Oswald's arrival at the rooming house was 1:04–1:05 p.m.; Tippit was killed somewhere between 1:14 and 1:16 p.m., nearly a mile away. The important question (discussed earlier) is whether there was enough time for Oswald to walk from his rooming house to the place where the policeman was murdered.

In the Texas theater where Oswald was captured, some claim that his gun had all six chambers loaded, which would have been unlikely if he had killed Tippit. George Applin of Dallas was sitting six rows from the rear of the movie theater and said that there was a person standing in the back row near him. Applin spoke to this person and said he had better move because someone up front had a gun, but that that person did not move. He didn't know who the individual was until two days later, and in 1979 he confessed to the *Dallas Morning News* that this other person was Jack Ruby. It seems clear that Ruby had come to the movie theater to meet Oswald.

There were absolutely no known notes for the twelve hours of questioning by the Dallas Police of Oswald, and a paraffin test on his hands and cheek was positive only for his hand, making it unlikely that Oswald had fired any kind of rifle. Such a positive result could also have come from the ink from the book cartons he usually handled in his job. Oswald's fingerprints were found on the rifle, and a palm print appeared on the loader, which Lt. J. O'Day, in charge of the fingerprint evidence, said had possibly been there for weeks or even months. At 7:30 a.m. on the day after the assassination a .38-caliber Smith & Wesson revolver similar to the one that Oswald owned was found in a brown paper bag near the grassy knoll. This fact was revealed only recently (2000), almost forty years after the crime. Further details of this FBI investigation still have not been released, and the significance of this revolver is uncertain. Now that the FBI has released only partial information about items found near the grassy knoll, one must wonder what other items were found and not reported.

Oswald's killer was Jack Ruby, who was in the jail area when Oswald was arraigned for the Tippit killing. At that time Oswald claimed that he was only the fall guy and had not killed anyone. Ruby had definite connections with the Mafia. Early in the 1920s and 1930s Ruby ran numbers for Al Capone and Frank Nitti of the Chicago mob. Then he went to Dallas in 1945 but worked with and for the Chicago mob, especially Jimmy Weisberg and Paul Labriola, two gunmen under Chicago don Sam Giancana. Ruby also was friends with Johnny Rosselli and his gang in Las Vegas and Mickey Cohen's group in Hollywood, California. He was also connected to Mafia bosses Santos Trafficante and Carlos Marcello. Ruby was also well acquainted with Dallas's Joe Campisi, who owned a restaurant where Ruby often ate, and Campisi was a close associate of Mafia don Carlos Marcello. British newsman John Wilson-Hudson reported that Ruby visited Santos Trafficante while Trafficante was in jail at Trescornia in Cuba. Thus Ruby had close ties to many prominent mob figures.

A few mysterious deaths provide evidence against the lone-gunman theory that claims Oswald killed Kennedy. For example, Melba Marcades, otherwise known as entertainer Rose Cheramie, was pushed out of a moving vehicle near Eunice, Louisiana, on November 20, 1963. The Louisiana State Police took her to the East Louisiana State Hospital, where she said that she had been thrown out of a car by two Latinos working for Jack Ruby; they had been sent to pick up some narcotics in Miami. She said that the president would be killed in Dallas in a few days. Later, after the assassination, when she read that Ruby claimed he had not known Lee Harvey Oswald, she said that Oswald had been in the Carousel Club many times and that the two were bedmates. Confirmation of their friendship came from dancer Beverly Oliver, who was introduced to Oswald by Ruby as Lee Oswald of the CIA. This story was buried until November 4, 1965, when Cheramie was killed by a car near Big Sandy, Texas; apparently she had been shot before being run over by the automobile. One other mysterious death was the suicide of Comdr. William B. Pitzer (USN), who had taken many photographs of Kennedy's brain. Earlier another officer (Daniel Marvin) had been approached by an unidentified individual to assassinate Pitzer in 1965 but refused (1992 Central TV Enterprises).

Another example can be found as a prediction for the assassination without any ties to Oswald. Right-winger Joseph Milteer and Willie Somersett can be heard on a tape made on November 9, 1963, anticipating a visit of Kennedy to Miami on November 18. Milteer said, "Kennedy is to be killed by a high-powered rifle from an office building." Furthermore, professional photographer and author Robert Groden has convincing photographic evidence that Milteer was in Dallas on November 22 among the spectators watching the president's motorcade.

Further ties between Ruby and Oswald and others help to make it unlikely that Lee Harvey Oswald was a lone nut looking for notoriety. Ruby seemed to know a great deal about Oswald, as he demonstrated when he corrected Dallas District Attorney Henry Wade who said that Oswald was a member of the Free Cuba committee; Ruby corrected the name to Fair Play for Cuba committee. How did Ruby know this unless he had some connection with Oswald? Ruby's excuse for why he shot Oswald was to protect the president's widow from the pain she would endure if she had to return for Oswald's trial. But this excuse was suggested by Ruby's attorney, Tom Howard. Ruby begged the Warren Commission to bring him to Washington, away from Dallas, where his life was in danger, so that he could tell the truth. He claimed that Lyndon Johnson was the power behind the assassination. In Ruby's polygraph test, only on the second time, did a large and suspicious galvanic skin response appear in his answer "No" to the important question, "Did you assist Lee Harvey Oswald in the assassination?" This is suggestive evidence that Ruby lied. Johnny Rosselli told well-known investigative reporter Jack Anderson that Ruby was a foot soldier for the mob. Ruby died in prison on January

3, 1967, of cancer. He had told his family that he was being injected with live cancer cells.

In a taped interview while in the Dallas jail, Ruby said, "The world will never know my motive and never know the true facts."

There are many other arguments against the lone-gunman theory and in favor of conspiracy. Presidential aide Kenneth O'Donnell rode in a Secret Service car and said that he heard a shot from the grassy knoll during the assassination. In another tie to the mob, Eugene (Braden) Brading, a Mafia associate with many convictions, was arrested and questioned in Dealey Plaza. It is interesting that he was present at both the John F. Kennedy and Robert F. Kennedy assassinations. Jack Martin was an investigator for Guy Banister's detective agency, but he was beaten by Banister when he started talking about visitors to the office, referring to Lee Harvey Oswald. This beating was well displayed in Oliver Stone's *JFK*. Martin also claimed that Banister and David Ferrie were both involved in the conspiracy to murder Kennedy. Some believe that Ferrie, an experienced pilot, was to fly the assassin away from Dallas, and it is interesting that on the day of the assassination, Ferrie was in Houston, Texas, where he claimed to be ice-skating.

On February 22, 1967, when he was about to be arrested for conspiracy in the president's murder, Ferrie died of a cerebral hemorrhage. Some investigators believe that Ferrie had been given an overdose of Proloid, a thyroglobulin, a purified extract of pig thyroid. The Physicians Desk Reference states that such drugs in large doses may "produce serious and even life threatening manifestations of toxicity." The postmortem photos showed a deep abrasion of the lower lip and lower face, as if Ferrie had been forced to ingest something like a drug that might have induced the hemorrhage. On the same day as Ferrie's death, Eladio delValle, whom Ferrie had said was his CIA paymaster, was murdered by a bullet in his heart and his head split open with an ax. District Attorney Jim Garrison of New Orleans investigated this murder.

In August 1968 a former roommate of Ferrie (Rev. Raymond Broshears) said that Ferrie was involved with Oswald. A man calling himself Harry Dean and claiming to be with the CIA and the FBI told writer W. R. Morris in 1976 that Oswald was not involved in the assassination, but that he had actually worked for the CIA and FBI. His relationship to the FBI can be found in one of their own documents, dated December 17, 1963, mentioning "Lee Harvey Oswald aka IS-R."

Summary

EVIDENCE AGAINST the lone-gunman theory is considerable. Oswald's ties to the mob include his close relationship with Charles "Dutz" Murret, who worked for Carlos Marcello, whose associate bailed Oswald out of jail. Another associate of Marcello was David Ferrie, who had contact with Oswald in the Civil Air Patrol, traveled with him to Clinton, Louisiana, and whose death was probably not a suicide. Jack Ruby had close ties to the mob, knew Oswald, may well have been in the theater when Oswald was captured, corrected the name of Oswald's group, and likely lied in his lie detector test. Guy Banister, who worked for the FBI and CIA, included his address on Oswald's pamphlets, and his secretary and investigator Jack Martin confirmed their relationship. Other evidence of Oswald's relationships with the FBI or CIA include the statements of his mother of such a relationship, his close friendship with DeMohrenschildt, the visit by the FBI while Oswald was in jail, payments from the FBI, and the destruction of Oswald's note to FBI agent Hosty. The involvement of the Dallas Police includes the patrol car signaling in front of Oswald's rooming house after the assassination and the absence of any notes of the interviews with Oswald while he was in jail.

Positive evidence of a conspiracy includes the meeting of Silvia Odio with Leon Oswald, claiming that an assassination would occur, and also statements from Joseph Milteer two weeks before and from Rose Cheramie two days before the assassination that the murder would take place. Other examples are Oswald's letter to Hunt, O'Donnell's statement about a shot from the grassy knoll, and inconclusive evidence of paraffin tests and fingerprints from Oswald.

Finally, the improbability that Oswald could have ever been the lone gunman includes the fact that he was a poor shot with a very cheap, misaligned rifle that was much longer than the curtain rods he brought to work. The assassination involved six to ten shots over a span of seven to eight seconds from a gun that was associated with a fake picture. If Oswald were the lone assassin, the firing on Elm Street rather than Houston Street made little sense, nor did his presence on the second floor of the depository one minute after the last shot, nor did his unhurried exit from the building. Finally, the evidence against Oswald for Tippit's killing is not at all convincing.

Addendum

BECAUSE OF the many controversies about Oswald, his wife, Marina, wanted to be certain that his casket actually contained his body. So the casket was dug up and opened in 1981. The mortician, Paul Rudy, claimed that the seal of the casket had been broken, but the teeth of the severed head were those of Oswald. But he also claimed there was no sign of an autopsy that he had expected would have been performed on the head. The mortician was left to wonder if Oswald's head had been later placed with the body in that casket.

15

The Real
Assassin

In 1989 INVESTIGATIVE REPORTER Joe West hoped to reopen the Kennedy assassination case and wanted to interview a prisoner in the Illinois State Penitentiary, our Deadeye, whose real name is James E. Files. West had learned about Files from FBI agent Zack Shelton. At first the prisoner was reluctant to be interviewed. But West finally gained Files's confidence just before West died suddenly in 1993. On March 22, 1994, associates of West conducted a taped interview with Files, who felt obligated to give such an interview, because he had developed a close relationship with West and had promised him an interview. This interview was called *Confessions of an Assassin*, which we possess.

Files had been a stock-car driver and then became the driver for Chuckie Nicoletti, one of Sam Giancana's gunmen in the Chicago Mafia. Files had identified Nicoletti as one of the best hit men under Giancana and Tony Accardo. Earlier Files had been involved with the training of Cuban refugees for the Bay of Pigs operation and felt strongly that Kennedy had been a traitor because he refused to allow the second wave of planes to depart from Nicaragua to protect the anti-Castro Cubans. Nicoletti was Files's boss and had indicated to him six months before the assassination that they were going to kill

John F. Kennedy and they were going to work with Johnny Rosselli in this hit. Files said that he had met with Rosselli through David Atlee Phillips, a senior member of the CIA and Files's controller. He also said that the first idea was to kill Kennedy in Chicago, but later discussions persuaded the mob to move the plan to Dallas.

One week before the Kennedy assassination Files drove a 1963 burgundy Chevrolet to Dallas; his immediate responsibility was to take care of the weapons. He stayed in the Lamplighter Inn on Downing Way in Mesquite, a suburb east of Dallas. Files claimed that Lee Harvey Oswald had come to his hotel, had driven around Dallas with him, and Files had also test-fired a weapon in the area. By November 21 everything had been set up in Dallas; Files understood the area well and had prepared the weapons appropriately. On the next day he went to Dallas, to the Cabana Hotel, which was supported by Hoffa's union and often patronized by the Mafia. At 7:00 a.m. he picked up Johnny Rosselli at the Cabana Hotel and went to Fort Worth to a pancake house on Route 30 and University Drive where they saw Jack Ruby. They went to the coffee shop, and there Ruby gave Rosselli a five-by-nine-inch envelope that included identification badges that seemed to be from the Secret Service and also a map showing the plan for the president's motorcade. After picking up Chuckie Nicoletti back at the Cabana Hotel, they proceeded to Dealey Plaza, arriving a few minutes before 10:00 a.m. After surveying the terrain at 10:30, Nicoletti asked Files to be one of the shooters.

The following describes Files's movements as he, Rosselli, and Nicoletti approached the motorcade route. Files parked the car beside the Dal-Tex Building across Houston Street from the Texas School Book Depository.

Nicoletti asked him, "Where would you position yourself in the Dealey Plaza?"

Files answered, "I would choose up there behind the tree beyond the stockade fence on the high ridge of the knoll. . . . I've got the railroad yard in back of me; we've got a parking lot there. I can pass myself off as a railroad worker for the time being, and when the time comes, nobody would really pay any attention to me. I would like to use the Fireball . . . it's easy to conceal and I can carry it in a briefcase and no one will notice me."

The physical layout of this area was advantageous for Files. The motorcade route down Elm Street had on its north side a grassy knoll extending 324 feet down to a triple underpass. Near the middle of the general area was a pergola, and the extension of this structure separated the grassy knoll into two parts. The south part was 190 feet long and extended 46 feet in width. Immediately behind the knoll was a picket fence 141 feet long and 5 feet high. Files would hide behind this fence, and the trees in front of the fence would further hide him; he would shoot between the trees and over the 5-foot fence. Behind him was a parking lot and a railroad spur; he wore a reversible plaid jacket as if he were a railroad worker. Thus Files was secure between the trees and behind the picket fence so that others could not easily see him. He would open the briefcase only when the motorcade was approaching. Anyone wishing to view the motorcade would have moved closer to Elm Street than where Files was positioned.

At 12:26 a.m. the motorcade approached. As Kennedy's car came near, Files zeroed in on the president's head, being careful not to hit his wife, Jacqueline. Nicoletti, in the Dal-Tex Building, fired from behind Kennedy, hitting him in the back of the head on the right. Just a fraction of a second later Files shot Kennedy on the right side of his head with a frangible bullet, violently thrusting him to his left.

Of the moments after the fatal shot, Files further related, "I put the Fireball back into the briefcase, closed it up, pulled my jacket off, reversed it so instead of the plaid side out, it would have gray side out, like a dress jacket. I put my hat on my head, walked away, carrying my briefcase." After the shot many viewers ran toward the grassy knoll, since many thought that a gunshot had come from there. Files was on his way out of the area by that time.

He walked to the Dal-Tex parking lot and found Nicoletti and Rosselli already in the car.

Files claimed that the shell casing of the bullet he fired had his teeth marks on it, and he placed this casing on the stockade fence on the grassy knoll. These teeth marks were his signature, later found in 1994, according to Files. Another item found on the day after the assassination near the grassy knoll by the FBI was a .38 revolver. This discovery was revealed only recently (2000), but the full report has not been released by the FBI. One wonders what else has been found by the FBI and not yet revealed. It is also interesting that, after the shooting, Dallas officer Joe Smith pulled a pistol on a man near the grassy knoll who then flashed a Secret Service identification card. But the Secret Service claimed not to have had any personnel in the area. It is not clear who Officer Smith encountered at that time. Files did not report that he had been involved in such an incident.

Rosselli had come out the side door of the Dal-Tex Building without a weapon. Nicoletti had carried out his gun, which was then placed in the trunk of the car. Files hit the accelerator. After making a right turn on Houston Street, they went five or six blocks, where another car was waiting for Nicoletti and Rosselli. Then Files returned to the Mesquite hotel. He said that he used hot wax to remove any gunpowder from his body. Later, he drove to Chicago, driving only during daylight hours with the weapons hidden behind the backseat. Files claimed that he was later paid thirty thousand dollars for this hit in Dallas.

Files said he met Lee Harvey Oswald in early 1963, when he was running guns for anti-Castro Cubans through David Atlee Phillips of the CIA. Files claims that Phillips was both his and Oswald's controller. He also had contact with Oswald in Clinton, Louisiana. Files claims that the CIA had a heavy hand in the assassination, had provided Secret Service identification documents for them, and also provided the Fireball weapon. The assassination was only the third time the gun was used; it was a product of an early CIA weapons-development program. Files said that it was designed in 1961, had a reinforced barrel, and used high velocity .221-caliber Remington bullets. It was a pistol ahead of its time and was effective even at one hundred yards. The Fireball used a fragmenting, exploding bullet with a mercury load, traveling at 3,100 feet per second with great penetration.

A very important question in the Kennedy assassination is why Kennedy's body was violently slammed to his left side after the right-sided head wound. Believers in the lone-gunman and single-bullet theories propose that a bullet entered the back of the head, coming from Oswald's rifle in the book depository behind the president. This bullet removed much of the right side of his brain, and some of the lone-gunman believers further propose that a reflex action accounts for the body being slammed to the opposite left side. As a professional neurophysiologist and forensic neurologist for nearly half a century, I (JRH) believe this is impossible. When I gave a lecture to both departments of neurology and neurosurgery at the University of Minnesota in 1997, some asked me after the lecture to comment on the Kennedy assassination. I then had the chance to get the combined opinion of these two departments as to whether they could explain the violent reaction to the left side as a reflex from blowing out much of the right hemisphere by the exploding bullet. Not a single member of either department agreed that that idea made any neurological sense.

When internationally renowned neurology experts like Dr. Louis Caplan of Harvard Medical Center discuss the effect of sudden, severe damage to the brain (like a hemorrhage, like Kennedy's brain injury), they emphasize that motor reactions on the other side of the body slowly develop in the form of a paralysis on that side. Furthermore, Dr. A. K. Ommaya described in his 1966 report in the annals of the Royal College of Surgeons of England that "the sequence of events [that occur] after a concussive blow was immediate general flaccidity [limpness], paralysis and areflexia [absence of reflexes]." Thus, neurology tells us that there is no reflex that can explain why Kennedy's body violently slammed to his left upon impact from a bullet to the right side of his brain. What does make sense is the obvious, namely, that a bullet from Kennedy's right side, the grassy knoll, drove him to his left with the great force of that bullet coming from his right. An exploding bullet from Kennedy's right side can be the only reasonable explanation of the violent thrust of his body to the left side. Dr. Vincent DiMaio, in his bible on gunshot wounds, explains that "a moving projectile by virtue of its movement possesses kinetic energy. As a bullet moves through the body it imparts kinetic energy to the surrounding tissue, flinging it away from the bullet's path."

Craig Roberts, former marine sniper and veteran police officer, in his book *Kill Zone*, said, "There was no question about it; John F. Kennedy had been shot from the right front"—from the grassy knoll. His experience in Vietnam taught him well about the kinetic energy behind a bullet driving the victim "away from the force." Anyone studying the Zapruder film can see the president's body being flung violently to his left. D. B. Thomas published in 2001 in *Science and Justice* a sophisticated and clever analysis of echo patterns and concluded that one shot definitely came from the grassy knoll.

Dr. James Stone, director of neurosurgery at Cook County Hospital in Chicago, often considered the murder capital of the United States, was asked to view the Zapruder in 1998 after a clearer version of the film was released. He probably has seen more gunshot wounds than any other neurosurgeon and has carefully studied their effects. Stone indicated to author JRH that he was already biased in favor of the lone-gunman and single-bullet theories because he had a highly respected colleague at the hospital who was a friend of the well-known pathologist (Dr. Michael Baden) who believed in these two theories. When Stone saw the violent and forceful movement of Kennedy's body to the left on impact from the bullet that splattered blood and brain tissue of his right hemisphere, he said, "That bullet had to come from the right side—the grassy knoll. Oswald was supposedly behind him, and a bullet from that direction could not produce that effect."

Furthermore, the bullet hole in Kennedy's back near his right shoulder blade made a small discrete hole (7 x 4 mm) and Army Lt. Col. Pierre Finck at the autopsy could not track that bullet hole for more than one inch. As photos have clearly shown, the bullet striking Kennedy's head removed much of the right hemisphere, and it is inconceivable that the same gun and same type bullet that left only a small discrete hole in the soft tissue of the back could also shatter the entire right side of the head. Files's frangible, exploding bullet explains the blown-out right hemisphere, and this bullet was the one that killed Kennedy. In his classic book on *Gunshot Wounds* DiMaio defines a frangible bullet as consisting of "bonded fragments of iron or lead that disintegrate on striking a hard surface. . . . [And] readily penetrate the human body." Again, the lone-gunman theory with one rifle and one type of bullet cannot explain the facts of the assassination.

Files claims that in Dallas, about forty to fifty feet from the grassy knoll, he saw Frank Sturgis and Eugene James Braden, both well-known mobsters. Files says that he knows who killed Dallas Officer J. D. Tippit. and it was not Oswald, but he refuses to identify the killer whom he believes is still alive. He indicates that Sam Giancana had given the orders to Nicoletti and was not sure whether or not Tony Accardo had given any orders to Giancana. Files also says that he knows how David Ferrie died of a brain hemorrhage but refuses to specify how the hemorrhage was induced.

Files claims he was born James E. Sutton in January 1942 in Alabama and later, for safety reasons, changed his name to Files. Early on he went to Chicago, where he grew up in the Italian section, running around with the wild kids of that area. In 1959 he became a member of the Eighty-second Airborne, and on July 10 of that year went to Laos as an adviser in small automatic weapons. He remained in that country for fourteen months. After returning to the United States, Files became a stock-car driver. Chuckie Nicoletti knew about his background, especially as an expert driver of vehicles and his knowledge of weapons, and included him as part of the Giancana family.

For the Dallas hit, Files said that Johnny Rosselli told him he had flown on a military air transport (MATS) plane from Washington DC to Dallas, which was arranged by the CIA. Files also said he knew Antonio Veciana, who was not involved in the assassination but was involved in the CIA. Veciana claimed that Maurice Bishop was Oswald's controller and that Bishop was really David Atlee Phillips. Files further claimed that, after the assassination, he was given a package from

Nicoletti that included Nicoletti's diary and the identification documents and maps from Dallas that had been given to them by Jack Ruby. He burned the latter two items but buried the diary. Later Files said that he was attacked, gassed, badly beaten, and interrogated by a group who wanted the diary. He thought it was more likely the CIA and not the mob that beat him up since he was still alive. The mob would have more likely killed him. He had a slow recovery from his injuries.

In June 1997 Antoinette Giancana wrote to Files in Joliet, Illinois, and asked if they could talk. It was reasonably assumed by the authors of this book that if Files were genuine in his story about his relationship with the Chicago mob and the hit in Dallas, he would likely respond. On the other hand, if his story had been made up and Files was a fraud, then he would not respond. But on July 1, 1997, Files wrote a very warm and cordial letter to Antoinette Giancana. This letter by itself strongly suggests that Files was in fact a member of the Chicago mob and that his story is credible. Since the James Files story is an embarrassment to the FBI and CIA, a number of individuals have told Antoinette Giancana that both of these organizations have tried to discredit him and have labeled him a phony. Even his military record, as part of the Eighty-second Airborne, was challenged, but Files provided documentation for us through John C. Grady, an airborne researcher, that he had indeed been attached to the Eighty-second Airborne. During a lengthy face-to-face interview, Antoinette was impressed by the clear details given by Files. He gave the name and telephone number of an individual who knew about his prior relationships with the Chicago mob. That individual (KL) with mob contacts proved to be the owner of a Chicago-area motel. Through her contacts, Antoinette Giancana talked with KL, who verified that James Files had been closely related to Chuckie Nicoletti and the Chicago mob.

Summary

James E. Files is in prison for life in Illinois, blamed for shooting a policeman. Joe West had learned of Files from a former FBI agent and was turned down often for an interview, but he later persuaded Files to talk with him. Because of a promise to West, Files permitted a videotaping of his interviews, even after West's untimely death. Files had been a stock-car driver and was a member of the Eighty-second Airborne, later working with the CIA in training anti-Castro Cubans for invasion of Cuba. His experience with stock cars led to his job as a driver for Chuckie Nicoletti, an important hit man in Sam Giancana's Chicago mob. Files discussed his drive to the Dallas area and meeting with Lee Harvey Oswald, Johnny Rosselli, and Jack Ruby. He was given Secret Service identification documents and picked up Nicoletti, who detailed Files to shoot Kennedy from the grassy knoll. Files had a weapon known as a Fireball, a handgun with a telescopic sight that used exploding, fragmenting bullets. He tells a very convincing story about his hit that removed nearly the whole right side of Kennedy's brain. This hit puts to rest the question of why Kennedy's body was thrown violently to his left side from the kinetic energy of the bullet from the grassy knoll. The CIA and FBI had obvious reasons to discredit Files, but a letter from Antoinette Giancana would likely settle whether Files was genuine; a response to her letter would verify his story. Antoinette Giancana traveled to the prison and interviewed Files, who was convincing about his role in the assassination. As further evidence in favor of Files's credibility, an interview by Antoinette Giancana with a motel owner with mob ties in Chicago verified Files's close relationships with Nicoletti and the Chicago mob. We firmly believe that James Files fired the head shot from the grassy knoll that killed President Kennedy.

16

Scrutiny of Deadeye

THIS CHAPTER WILL DEAL with the positive and negative features of the statements made by James E. Files. At this time, decades after the Kennedy assassination, anyone who comes forward with any theory or with any evidence will be viewed with great skepticism by many different groups of investigators who have had years to solidify their own views. First, the media are known to be liberal and usually favor the lone-gunman theory. The media generally discredit any conspiracy theory about the assassination of Kennedy and vilify those who write about such plots. One reason for such a position is that it is more favorable and comforting to the media to suppose that a lone individual like Lee Harvey Oswald killed Kennedy rather than admit that a group of powerful forces had understandable reasons for wanting the president dead.

Still, one can find many references to Files on the Internet. It is impressive how much heat rather than light has been shed upon the possibility that he may have been involved in Kennedy's death. We are reminded that when we discuss topics without definite answers, like sex or religion, there is usually an inverse relationship between how much emotion we feel and how much proof we can provide. The FBI and the CIA have their own interests in discrediting any evidence that would favor a conspiracy, because this implies that they failed in their responsibilities. After all, who can stop a lone gunman? But an organized conspiracy could and should have been stopped. Government protective agencies certainly would prefer the lone-gunman theory to explain the assassination rather than admit that different groups who wanted the president dead came together to bring about his murder. For example, FBI agent Zack Shelton, with twenty-eight years of service, who had spent six to seven years on the Chicago crime scene, knew that James Files was closely associated with Chuckie Nicoletti. He had long believed that Nicoletti, Rosselli, and Giancana were in some way involved in the assassination of John F. Kennedy. Shelton went so far as to give Joe West the lead on Files. Not only did Shelton risk his job but also his pension by conveying the information to West, who then contacted James Files.

To check Files's credibility let us review briefly the people behind the videotape of Files's statement. First, Joe West was a former Baptist minister who became involved with fund-raising for various church activities and actually received some credit for helping well-known evangelist Jim Bakker to get his prison sentence reduced. After his religious activities, West became a private investigator who had a lot of flash and jewelry. His attempt to sell shares in the Files story was cut short by heart surgery in Houston. He died suddenly of an infection in a Houston County hospital in 1993.

Bob Vernon was Joe West's producer, and he took over the story after West's death, trying to persuade others to invest twenty thousand dollars in the effort to bring the Files story to the public. Vernon was unable to follow through with the Files story, suffered a financial disaster, and sold the rights of this story to MPI, which is associated with well-known entertainer Dick Clark. Clark's producer, Barry Adelman, was not able to collaborate with West's researchers. The MPI organization did, however, produce the tape with the Files confession. Although Dick Clark has a positive reputation in the eyes of the American public and was behind the MPI organization, some of the past problems of getting this story out affected its impact. Therefore, the Files story remains essentially unknown to the American public. We stumbled upon it accidentally.

A major question is whether Files is a fraud who wants only to draw attention to himself; he may not have been involved in the assassination at all. If Files wanted only attention, it is hard to understand why he would have told Joe West he wanted nothing to do with him and refused to see him. Only much later did he open up, but he said he "didn't want to be a part of history" and that he was "only following orders in Dallas." Another major point is that if James E. Files were a complete fraud and had nothing to do with the assassination, the letter from Antoinette Giancana would obviously have gone unanswered. If he were telling the truth, then he would likely answer her letter. That he did reply in a warn and affectionate way weighs in his favor. The facts of the assassination plot will never be established to everyone's comfort level of confidence. What we can do, however, is apply common sense and reason to the situation. In this instance it is common sense that answering Giancana's letter and meeting with her adds great credibility to Files. He had no obligation to reply to her and would likely not have done so if he were a fraud.

Some have questioned Files's military background because he claims he was part of the Eighty-second Airborne. John C. Grady of Friend Finders Services, also of the Eighty-second Airborne, confirms that Files was part of this unit. Files claims he was in Laos to train troops in that territory. Some argue that this could not have occurred, because Files would have been only seventeen or eighteen years old, and the military would obviously not have used him in this way. But it is perfectly clear that in times of crisis, young or poorly trained individuals are sometimes sent overseas to fight or train, especially in a country like Laos, where the U.S. government had its own hidden agenda. The military does not wait for the most experienced individuals to serve in that particular capacity. As a colonel in the U.S. Army Reserves, serving in Germany, where we were sending troops to move on to Desert Storm, I (JRH) saw many young soldiers about to go into that war.

Others claim that there are no military records on James E. Files to confirm his story. We now know one major reason why his history is not available in the usual army personnel records. Files claimed that he had served in White Star teams in Laos. Col. Fletcher Prouty knows of the White Star teams, and he has stated that when army personnel were reassigned to serve as trainers in Laos, their records were usually pulled from the army personnel folders and transferred to special army intelligence files. Thus it is a problem for anyone to verify Files's military record. Prouty has indicated that these teams were "sheep dipped," that is, hired by a private company created by the CIA and sent to Laos to train troops. One army major pointed out that if James Files were a phony, how would he know about the White Star teams since they are not well known even among career military personnel? Kennedy researcher James Marrs makes this latter point very clear. Marrs also makes the point that Files knew about the abort team, mentioned to him by Johnny Rosselli, that was supposed to disrupt any attempted assassination of Kennedy. Fearing for his own safety, Rosselli may have declined to take part in the shooting, so Nicoletti had asked Files to be part of the assassination team. The possibility of an abort team was not common knowledge, and it would seem that Files's awareness of such a team would require information from someone like Rosselli.

Files could be challenged in his claim that he had contacts with some well-known individuals such as David Atlee Phillips, a high-profile CIA agent in the Caribbean area and, according to Files, his controller. Files added that Oswald was also under Phillips's control, and certainly there are many reasons to believe that Oswald had an association with the CIA as well as the FBI. There is a well-known story about an individual calling himself Maurice Bishop, who was seen with Oswald as claimed by Antonio Veciana, a friend of Files. Since photographs of each indicate it is likely that Bishop was Phillips, Files is probably correct that Oswald and Phillips knew each other. Furthermore, Files's claim that he met Richard Helms of the CIA could be challenged, especially since the deputy director was not Helms but Lt.

Gen. Marshall Carter at the time when Files believed the two had met. Helms, of course, later became director of the CIA, and possibly the problem is a matter of the meeting dates, which are often not clear in anyone's mind decades later. The position of the present authors is not to be apologists for any inaccuracy of James Files but to be reasonable about his general accuracy.

One possible inconsistency in Files's story is that he said Johnny Rosselli told him he had flown into Dallas from Washington DC on a Military Air Transport Service flight arranged by the CIA, but it seems possible that it did happen. As an officer on active duty, I (JRH) have flown on MATS flights that had civilians aboard and know that this does occur. But William Robert "Posh" Plumlee was a pilot who said he had flown from Florida to New Orleans on November 21, 1963, and then back to Dallas after picking up a "Col." Johnny Rosselli. Did Rosselli come from Washington DC on a MATS flight or did Plumlee bring him to Dallas from New Orleans? Files only reported what Rosselli told him and cannot be held accountable for any of Rosselli's incorrect statements or misrepresentations.

Some critics may take Files to task in his claim that Lee Harvey Oswald was able to drive a car because he did not have a license, a fact known by Files. It is also clear that most individuals in the service (and Oswald was in the marines) learned to drive vehicles, especially Jeeps. Therefore, it is likely Oswald was able to drive a vehicle even though he did not have a license. Files also maintained he had been with Oswald in New Orleans in 1963. One critic has tried to discredit Files, claiming he said he met Oswald in 1961, but at that time Oswald was still in Minsk. Files, however, said they met in 1963, not 1961.

Why was Files told only two hours before the assassination attempt that he would be one of the shooters. Since Mafia hits are well planned, it would be uncommon that there would be such a short interval between the announcement of the plan and the actual event. But a twenty-one-year-old would be expected to be very nervous about the possibility that he would be part of an assassination team to kill the president if he knew ahead of time. It is also possible that

Rosselli was to be one of the shooters, then after hearing about an abort team from the government that was to focus on possible assassins, he realized he could be doomed if he were caught and so chose not to participate. Therefore it is entirely possible that at the last moment the Mafia needed another shooter and called upon Files, who was known to be an accurate marksman.

The Fireball is a handgun with a telescopic sight, and it is known that Files owned such a weapon, only that it was a later model than the one likely used in the assassination. Also, there is evidence that David Atlee Phillips had given Files that Fireball weapon. Files also claimed that the weapon had used frangible .221 shots with a mercury load, which would certainly have produced major damage. Anyone viewing the Zapruder film can see how this head shot removed a large part of the right side of Kennedy's head. One argument about Files's account is that he claimed to be watching through the Fireball's scope and was still able to describe what occurred. But it is clear that this weapon has a tremendous kick, and the question is whether or not he could see anything through the scope at the time the strike occurred. It is also clear that there was a great shower of blood, brain, and skull, and anyone looking in Kennedy's direction would have seen the result of this blast. Some critics maintain that the Fireball makes such a loud noise that there would have been claims of a shot heard from the grassy knoll. In fact, there were many individuals who claimed that a shot had come from that location. Another question was why no one in the Dal-Tex Building said that they heard shots from that building, although Nicoletti claimed to have been a shooter there. One can easily imagine with such mass confusion, particularly after a number of shots rang out, that it was difficult to know where shots were coming from because of echo effects in the canyon of buildings. One last criticism was that the Remington Arms Corporation apparently indicated that its Fireball XP-100 used .221 and not .222 shells, and so Files was wrong in claiming that it was a .222 shell. But Files is clear that he used a .221 bullet in a .222 casing.

A very important point that adds to the credibility of James E.

Files is his claim that he took the shell from the bullet that killed Kennedy and bit down on it so that his teeth marks were on the casing and left it on a post at the grassy knoll. John C. Rademacher of Granbury, Texas, found a casing in 1987 and brought it to investigator Jim Marrs's class at the University of Texas at Arlington in 1990. On May 3, 1993, Bob Vernon and Barry Adelman of the MPI group interviewed Files when Files said that his teeth marks were on this shell. Two months later (July) Bob Vernon and Joe West's widow visited Rademacher to discuss the matter. Five months after Files claimed that his teeth marks were on the shell, we have a statement from Dr. Paul Stimson of the University of Texas at Houston and a member of the American Board of Oral Pathology and Forensic Odontology. His statement dated October 4, 1993, comments: "The indentations are oriented on the shell casing in a pattern that would be consistent with the maxillary right central incisor making the larger mark and two smaller marks would be consistent with the lower right central and lateral incisors. It is my opinion that the marks are consistent with having been made by human indentation." West had talked with Rademacher a year before he met Files, and he had photos of the dented cartridge when he visited Files in prison. The major point here is that there should be no way Files could have known there were teeth marks on the shell casing unless he had placed them there. After all, his interview of May 3, 1993, was five months prior to Stimson's statement. A devil's advocate may say that Files could have heard from someone that the cartridge was dented, but in fact he could not have known that the indentations were teeth marks unless he put them there. There are, however, two problems about this matter. The first is that a second shell casing was allegedly also found. The other problem is that shells were presumably found on both sides of the pergola pedestals about fifteen feet from where Abraham Zapruder stood and not exactly in the area where Files had claimed he had stood (fifteen feet from the end of the picket fence). But there are many ways in which shell casings can be moved over a period of years by winds, lawn mowers, and such, but it is not at all clear why another shell casing could be found. One claim is that the FBI agents "salted" the area with various kinds of shell casings.

Some critics say that Files is wrong in his claim that he saw mobsters James Braden and Frank Sturgis at the assassination site. According to the report of the House Assassination Committee (pp. 260–61), Sturgis was not there, but many investigators have noted a close resemblance between him and one of the tramps photographed in the railroad yard behind the grassy knoll. Many investigators had said Braden (Brading) was there, and in fact, Braden was picked up by a Dallas sheriff's deputy near the book depository right after the assassination. He was later released. A final point is that Files says that he returned to the Mesquite motel and took care of the guns that were used, because that was his original responsibility. Some critics claim that it was unprofessional of him to haul these guns in and out of the car trunk, but that may well have been done in an appropriate and subtle way.

This concludes a discussion regarding the credibility of James E. Files and his description of the events that had occurred in Dallas. We firmly believe that Files is not a fraud and that nearly all of his claims are correct.

The most important point in this chapter, however, will come from studying the new, clear version of the Zapruder film that was produced in 1998. When one follows it frame by frame in slow motion, one can see the body of Kennedy being violently slammed to his left side when the bullet struck the right side of his head. The only way such a violent movement can be explained is that a shot came from his right side onto his right temple area, imparting kinetic energy to slam the body to the left. No neurological reflex can account for such a body movement if one assumes that shots might have come from behind Kennedy (from the book depository) into his right hemisphere; this explanation will not hold. From an interview with Christian David, a claim was made in 1992 (Nigel Turner Productions) that a person (Lucien Satee), referred to as Badge-man from the Corsican Mafia, was also a shooter behind the picket fence, and a puff of smoke, as if from a gun, from that area has been described by some witnesses. Also, testimony from Dallas citizen Gordon Arnold was that a shot from the grassy knoll whizzed past his left ear. A further claim was that the Corsican Mafia group was met in Brownsville, Texas, by Giancana's Chicago group, who took them to Dallas. The authors of this book maintain that anyone who views the slow-motion version of the Zapruder film will conclude the head shot must have come from the grassy knoll area, and if the shooter was not Files, it was someone else near to him. We strongly believe that it was James Files.

17

Kennedy and Giancana: Relationships and Speculations

W<small>HAT IS THE EVIDENCE</small> for a CIA hit against Sam Giancana?

One theory mentioned in various books is that the mob assassinated one of its own: Sam Giancana. The motivation is supposedly that some of them were upset that Giancana had collected a great deal of money from his international casino business while he lived in Mexico and did not share those profits with the Mafia. That possibility seems very unlikely because it was Giancana's own business after his retirement from the Mafia, unrelated to the rest of the mob. Furthermore, the Mafia certainly would have no reason to care whether or not Giancana was involved in the Cuban connection with the attempted assassination of Fidel Castro and, instead, would have understood that the government had hired him to do a job the government could not or chose not to do. The timing of Giancana's expected appearance before the Church Committee should also have made no difference to the mob. Therefore, the possibility that the mob had any motivation to eliminate Giancana seems dubious.

Many investigators have concluded that Giancana was killed by a fellow mobster, since there was no sign of forced entry, meaning that he must have let the killer into his home. We have learned from daughter Antoinette that there was always an unlocked door to the basement where Giancana was killed, and therefore, that assumption that the killer must have been known to him is wrong. Only because Butch Blasi was one of the last to see Giancana alive was he under suspicion. Blasi returned to the Giancana home with his daughter, Connie Sue, who loved her "Uncle" Sam; more important, Blasi was like a son to Sam Giancana. The Giancana family believes very strongly that Blasi could not have done this.

The evidence for CIA involvement in Giancana's death includes the fact that lobbyist Fred Black, a Washington insider, had warned Johnny Rosselli the night before his murder that he should leave the Florida area at once, because he knew that Rosselli's life was in jeopardy. Unfortunately, Rosselli did not take his advice and was murdered in Tampa. Black had many contacts with the CIA and likely learned from these connections that Rosselli was about to be murdered. Although a weak case could be made that the mob believed Rosselli might have been talking too much to reporters, no group other than the CIA had any reason to kill Rosselli. It is also likely that the CIA planned the Giancana killing, since the two assassinations seem to be closely related. After all, Rosselli testified before the Church Committee and was killed, and Giancana was killed before he was able to testify before this same committee about the attempted assassination of Castro.

One important fact is that the three cars that were always outside Giancana's home—one from the CIA, one from the FBI, and one from the Oak Park Police—all had left the premises together near the time of the murder. Before that night the drivers of these cars had always alternated their breaks. They all returned just after the murder was called in by the housekeeper. This fact does implicate the CIA, because neither the local Oak Park Police nor the FBI had any obvious reason to kill Giancana. The sudden disappearance of these three cars at the same time could never have been ordered by the Mafia, and this one fact makes perfectly clear that the mob was not involved.

There is the fact that Charles Grimaldi told author John Kidner that the murder was a CIA hit, and Grimaldi, of course, was one of the mobsters whose business would justify his knowing such things. Perhaps the most important point of all was the timing of this murder, namely, on the night when staffers from the Church Committee arrived in Chicago to escort Giancana back to Washington DC to testify to the committee. The fact that Giancana was murdered the night before he was to travel and then appear before the committee is very compelling. Other authors have indicated that Johnny Rosselli and Robert Maheu had given testimony to the committee on the attempted assassination, and therefore such testifying would not motivate the CIA to eliminate Giancana because he would not add any significant details. But these other two individuals testified after Giancana was to appear before the committee. Therefore, the CIA could not have known what Rosselli and Maheu might say and had reason to be very concerned about what Giancana would say.

There are some authors who claim that the CIA would not dare murder Giancana. The point needs to be emphasized that the same agency had targeted five heads of state and had been associated indirectly with the murders of four of them. That the CIA would target a gangster whose testimony might embarrass it is consistent with its murdering business during the 1960s and 1970s. Perhaps the most compelling evidence of all that the hit on Giancana was not by the Mafia but by the CIA was the call from James "Cowboy" Mirro to Robert McDonnell, Antoinette's husband, that the Mafia had not been the ones to hit Sam Giancana.

What is the evidence that the mob and the CIA were involved in the assassination of John F. Kennedy?

First, there are fourteen links between the Kennedy family and the Chicago mob, most involving John F. Kennedy and Sam Giancana. The evidence that Sam Giancana was involved includes the strong motivation he had to eliminate President Kennedy because of the obvious double cross after the presidential election. Giancana had played a major role in the 1960 presidential primaries and especially in delivering Illinois, which was crucial for Kennedy's election. Yet Kennedy broke many promises to Giancana after he was elected, though his election was in part through the efforts of the Chicago mob. Giancana would have had extra motivation because he was forced to make arrangements for an abortion for one of his girlfriends, Judith Campbell, who had allegedly been made pregnant by Kennedy.

Giancana sent fellow mobsters Chuckie Nicoletti and Richard Cain to Dallas as shooters. We note that James Files was under the direct supervision of Nicoletti and was the shooter firing from the grassy knoll. All the evidence indicates that Files's story is internally consistent and generally correct. Finally, we have testimony from Giancana's half brother that Sam claimed "We took care of Kennedy," and testimony from his daughter, Antoinette, that Sam had said the Kennedys "would get their lunch." Sam also made many comments to Antoinette about his great hatred for the president.

Then we have the evidence from Santos Trafficante. Trafficante sent two Cuban exiles to Dallas as shooters. As motivation, he had a casino and hotel empire in Havana, which he lost and never recovered after Castro came to power. Then the Bay of Pigs invasion failed, President Kennedy's cancellation of the second wave of bombers from Nicaragua. Some very clear evidence comes from Frank Ragano, Trafficante's attorney, who made it clear that he carried the message from Hoffa to Trafficante that Kennedy had to be eliminated and that he heard the dying Trafficante say that perhaps they should have killed Robert F. Kennedy rather than John F. Kennedy, since Robert F. Kennedy had caused so much trouble for the mob.

Finally, we have evidence from Carlos Marcello, who had the greatest motivation of all. Robert F. Kennedy had made the arrangements for him to be kidnapped from a New Orleans office and sent into the jungles of San Salvador and Honduras, where Marcello underwent a great ordeal and almost died before he returned to civilization. It was Marcello who sent Charles Harrelson and Jack Lawrence as part of the group to Dallas to assassinate Kennedy. Lawrence was an expert marksman, and Harrelson is presently in jail for killing Judge John Wood and has been identified by some as one of the tramps in the railroad yard. Recently (2001), on national television, Harrelson admitted that he did, in fact, resemble one of the hobos photographed in the railroad yard near the assassination site. The most important evidence from Marcello comes from his colleague, Ed Becker, who reported that Marcello indicated, "If you want to kill the dog, you don't cut off his tail, you cut off his head," referring to the fact that John F. Kennedy would be the targeted one, not Robert F. Kennedy. Finally, Marcello's son knew about the assassination before it occurred. These three mob leaders, therefore, had their own motivations to eliminate Kennedy, and the evidence is clear, particularly in statements from their colleagues, that they were involved in the president's assassination.

The evidence that the CIA was involved in the Kennedy assassination derives from the organizations ire against the president. Kennedy had fired Director Allen Dulles, Director of Covert Operations Richard Bissell, and Deputy Director Charles Cabell. The president indicated that he was going to downgrade the importance of the CIA, blaming the agency for the disaster at the Bay of Pigs. One of Kennedy's national security memos indicated that the CIA was going to be removed from all cold-war operations and this responsibility would be given to the Joint Chiefs of Staff. This move demoted the CIA. The organization had planned the murders of five heads of state and was indirectly responsible for four of them. Therefore it is not surprising that it was involved in some way in the assassination of another head of state—Kennedy. The CIA's E. Howard Hunt was spotted by some in Dealey Plaza, and this provides more evidence that the CIA was involved. In Dallas, James Files claimed to have seen Frank Sturgis, who had worked with Johnny Rosselli in the mob but also was involved with the CIA and with Hunt in the Watergate fiasco. Finally, David Atlee Phillips, a major CIA player, was the controller of Files (according to him) and also of Lee Harvey Oswald (according to Files and others). The evidence for CIA involvement is indirect and circumstantial, but rogue elements from this agency were greatly motivated to eliminate Kennedy. Veteran FBI agent Zack Shelton said that rogue elements of the CIA together with the mob were likely responsible for the Kennedy assassination.

The most important point in this book is what happened to the president's body when the bullet struck the right hemisphere of his brain. In the latest version of the Zapruder film, Kennedy's body slammed to the left side after this bullet strikes. Those interested in promoting the lone-gunman theory had an "explanation" in response to the blasting away of the right hemisphere, namely that there was some kind of neurological reflex to explain this sudden move to the left side of Kennedy's body. Also, they theorized the splattering of his right hemisphere helped to produce a jet effect to account for the left-ward thrust. But there is no question that this kind of reflex does not exist, and one cannot explain the violent thrust of the body to the left side by any such means. The policeman on Kennedy's left (Patrolman Bobby Hargis), not on the right side, was splattered with the president's blood. So such a "jet effect" is not valid. Such an effect would demand that blood and brain would be sprayed to the right side, but it was to the opposite side, to the left. There is only one way to explain this movement: the obvious kinetic energy of a shot from the right side, namely from the grassy knoll, forcing the body in the direction of the bullet. Therefore, there had to be at least one shooter other than those who were behind the president in the book depository or the Dal-Tex Building. The evidence is clear that there had to be a shooter on the grassy knoll, and we believe we have interviewed him—James Files. This, we think, is the most crucial point that argues very strongly against a single shooter positioned behind the president.

During a radio interview, Zack Shelton made an appeal for some kind of confirmation that the claim of James Files is genuine. We have provided this confirmation.

One of the issues raised in this book that needs further discussion is a final thought on the link between the assassinations of President Kennedy and Sam Giancana. We have identified fourteen links between the two men. One issue that ties together those two killings and the thread that we've followed here deals with the CIA. This agency had planned the Bay of Pigs invasion and believed that Kennedy was responsible for its failure. Rather than admit to this, he blamed the

CIA, threatened to downgrade its importance, and fired the major players. Through various national security action memos, he downgraded the agency. As a result, rogue elements in the CIA were ready to aid in Kennedy's removal. This same agency had engaged in assassination plots against foreign heads of state. This fact was exposed by the Church Committee, which then scheduled Sam Giancana to testify. The plan for Giancana's group to assassinate Castro resulted in a hoax; Giancana and his colleagues never intended to carry out the killing. Giancana's plan, but especially his failure to kill Castro, were certainly an embarrassment for the CIA, which did not want Giancana to testify before the committee. Thus, the CIA's plan to involve Giancana in the attempt to kill Castro set Giancana up for his own assassination.

The CIA was able to pull off the other assassinations, but not with Castro, despite all of its efforts, all the money that went into it, and all of the players involved. It's somewhat surprising that Castro survived twenty-four assassination attempts. The money exchanges did occur, and the Kennedy administration expected that the money given to Giancana would buy Castro's murder. In fact, there is some suggestion from the recent book by investigator Gus Russo that Trafficante, to facilitate illicit drug trafficking, was actually telling Castro or back-channeling to him information about the CIA's attempts to kill him. Thus, Castro likely was forewarned. Not only did Castro have information provided by the Cuban exile community, but he also seemed to know what the CIA was doing in general. He may well have had the advantage of the Soviet spy system in the United States, because the Soviets had close military and political ties with Cuba. Another issue is whether there was a concern over protecting the Mafia drug traffic through Havana to Miami at that time. Was that drug operation at risk somehow in the Kennedy plan to assassinate Castro?

A strong tie between the Kennedy and Giancana assassinations is the thread of CIA involvement, and that thread becomes even stronger when we consider that Giancana's half brother Chuck indicated Sam's continued involvement with the CIA while living in Mexico but traveling worldwide. In these activities Sam could well have been a contact man or lead man in making bribes, deals, and connections for the CIA. If this were the case, as suggested in Chuck's book *Double Cross,* then the CIA would have another concern about Giancana's testimony before the Church Committee.

In some of the books on the Kennedy assassination, especially those favoring the lone-gunman theory, the point is made that, if there were any kind of conspiracy, then it surely would be known by this time. The fact is that we have learned a great deal about this conspiracy. Its many murders, especially those committed by the Mafia, have gone unsolved. Secrets are often buried with the individuals who are assassinated, and it is possible at this time and at other times in history to have a conspiracy without all the details becoming known.

We've speculated on how a conspiracy of this magnitude could be set up and who would actually have coordinated such a plan. The qualifications and requirements of the coordinator for this assassination would need to be special. Such an individual would need long service as a coordinator and a commitment to secrecy with access to, not just the FBI and CIA, but also a range of intelligence associations in our government. These would include the Office of Naval Intelligence and the Defense Intelligence Agency, as well as private security companies that usually hire retired members from these latter organizations. Furthermore, secrecy would have to be a step beyond even the top-secret status of these bureaucracies, which usually have enough leakage that almost everything would have been leaked by now. Therefore, we have to look at the supersecret counterintelligence groups within these agencies to find the level of security necessary to pull off such a conspiracy.

The one person who could coordinate such a conspiracy would be, in our opinion, J. Edgar Hoover. The reason for the choice of Hoover is his long history, his fame and his "ideological" strength and power in this country. In addition, his determination to avoid forced retirement and his hatred of the Kennedys equaled or exceeded that of any other person with a motive for the assassination. A small central organizing committee among counterintelligence groups within the government would be absolutely necessary, because if only one organization were involved, it would inevitably become known to other groups. Hoover as the leader of such a group would consider the actions of both Robert F. Kennedy and John F. Kennedy as irresponsible, certainly during the Cuban missile crisis. Robert F. Kennedy's actions would appear to violate every principle of negotiation and good government in the eyes of such a group. John F. Kennedy's liaisons with many individuals of questionable background would look like a violation of respect, confidentiality, and secrecy within the government. A Hoover-controlled counterintelligence committee would look upon the Kennedy brothers as government employees who consistently violated their oaths of office. Thus Hoover could well have been a coordinator for such a conspiracy and could feel justified in his action. We have made this suggestion without any proof and have realized that the public will likely find it shocking and unbelievable. We were surprised ourselves when we recently viewed a movie (*Silencers*) about the FBI that included the point that Hoover may have coordinated the assassination.

Other forces that were enemies of John F. Kennedy were the military-industrial complex, especially after Kennedy awarded the huge TFX contract for political rather than military reasons. Also, NSAM memos make it clear that Kennedy planned to withdraw from Vietnam, and the war machine providing the guns and ammunition then became an even stronger enemy to the president.

We have made clear that the lone-gunman theory involving Lee Harvey Oswald is completely false, as is the single-bullet theory. Finally, we have introduced to you the man who killed John F. Kennedy. His name is James Files.

Appendix

TIME LINE

DATE	EVENT
1908	June 15: Sam Giancana (**SG**) born
1910	February 6: Carlos Marcello (**CM**) born
1914	November 14: Santos Trafficante Jr. (**ST**) born
1919	Joseph P. Kennedy (**JPK**) manager of stockbroker firm
1923	SG called "Mooney," worked for Diamond Joe Esposito
1928	June: SG feared and respected by community
1929	JPK manipulates stock market crash
1934	President Franklin D. Roosevelt (**FDR**) appoints JPK head of Securities and Exchange Commission JPK into movie industry backed by mob unions
1936	Carlos Marcello into New Orleans Mafia
1937	FDR appoints JPK ambassador to Great Britain SG impresses Mafia bosses Purple Gang contract on JPK, saved by Esposito
1940	JPK resigns as ambassador
1942	Accardo appointed boss by Paul Ricca in Chicago mob January: James Files (**JF**) born
1944	Meyer Lansky persuades Fulgencio Batista to quit politics
1945	Jack Ruby moves to Dallas
1946	ST owns Havana casinos December: SG as national Mafia figure in mob
1947	Lucky Luciano appoints Meyer Lansky as "regent" in Cuba John F. Kennedy (**JFK**) marries Durie Malcolm

APPENDIX

1948   CM boss of New Orleans Mafia
Millions invested in Cuba casinos by SG

1952   Batista in power in Cuba
Lansky helps Batista become dictator in Cuba

1953   CM buys Town & Country Motel as headquarters

1954   August 11: Santos Trafficante Sr. dies and son takes over

1955   July: Lee Harvey Oswald (**LHO**) contacts David Ferrie
CM buys Churchill Farms
SG appointed boss of Chicago mob
Col. Fletcher Prouty named chief of special operations with Joint Chiefs
     of Staff (holds office until 1964)

1956   May: JPK to SG to remove his contract placed by Frank Costello

1957   January 30: Robert F. Kennedy (**RFK**) on Senate committee investigating
organized crime
November 14: Mafia meets in Appalachin, NY
November 27: J. Edgar Hoover (**JEH**) launches Top Hoodlum Program
ST meets JFK in Havana, Cuba
Antoinette Giancana has two dates with Bebe Rebozo

1958   December 31: Castro seizes power in Cuba

1959   March: CM defiant in McClellan Senate Committee
March 24: RFK asks why CM not deported
June 8: ST declared alien in Cuba
July 10: JF with Eighty-second Airborne in Laos
August 18: ST released from Cuba
November: Visit by JPK to SG
December 11: CIA director Allen W. Dulles approves Castro assassination

1960   January: SG to Frank Sinatra to start work on JFK election
February 7: Sinatra introduces JFK to Judith Campbell
April: JFK gives large amount of cash to Judith Campbell to deliver to SG
July: JFK briefed on Cuba by CIA
August: JFK sends more money to SG through Judith Campbell
September: JFK briefed on Cuba by Alabama governor John Patterson
Rosselli and Maheu meet in Beverly Hills, California
Rosselli, Maheu, and CIA support chief meet
October 1960: Bug in entertainer Dan Rowan's room
November 4: CIA cable to proceed with training for Bay of Pigs invasion

Time Line

November 8: Many calls to SG from Frank Sinatra regarding the election
December: Patrice Lumumba arrested in the Congo
CIA supplies anti-Trujillo forces in Dominican Republic

1961 January: JEH denies Mafia existence
January 17: Lumumba murdered
February: Poison pills delivered to SG team to kill Castro
February 13: Exploding cigars for Castro delivered to SG
March 15: RFK orders expulsion of CM
April: More supplies sent to anti-Trujillo forces
April 4: CM kidnapped, sent to Guatemala
April 15: First air attack in Cuba but three planes remain on the ground
April 16: 1:45 p.m.: Final tactical plan for Cuba approved by JFK
  9:30 p.m.: Bundy instructs CIA not to launch planned air strike
April 17: Bay of Pigs disaster
April 18: Maheu tells FBI about Rowan tap
April 19: CIA contacts White House about Alabama pilots
April 21: JFK states no more questions about Cuba
April 22: JFK contacts Gen. Maxwell Taylor regarding failure of Bay of Pigs
April 24: JFK blames CIA for Bay of Pigs
April 28: JFK and SG meet in Judith Campbell's room
May 7: Rosselli and SG offered money to kill Castro
May 9: RFK informs JEH of offer to pay Mafia
May 30: Rafael Trujillo murdered
June: Meeting between JFK and Nikita Krushchev
June 2: CM returns to the United States
June 6: Memo from Kennedy liaison to FBI about hiring Mafia to kill
  Castro
June 13: General Taylor submits report on Bay of Pigs
June 28: National Security Action Memo (**NSAM**) no. 55
July 11: Defense Intelligence Agency established
CM ordered deported
August 8: Two women in Judith Campbell's room for JFK
Microphones in Armory Lounge to monitor SG
September: John A. McCone named CIA director
November 16: JFK claims he is against assassinations
CIA Operation Mongoose begins as covert action against Castro
December 4: JEH tells RFK about secret donations by SG for JFK
December 9: FBI tapes SG
December 10: CM free on bond

APPENDIX

1962 January:: FBI tapes SG
January 19: RFK says Cuba top priority
January 29: CIA squashes prosecution of Rowan wiretap case
February 19: Richard Helms succeeds Richard Bissell as CIA director
February 27: JEH memo to RFK reveals he knows about Judith
Campbell
March 22: JEH lunch with JFK regarding Judith Campbell
March 23: JFK breaks with Sinatra
April: CIA's William Harvey passes poison pills to Johnny Rosselli
April 4: George Krutilek's body found regarding Billy Sol Estes scam in
Texas
May: Possible impeachment of Vice President Lyndon B. Johnson (**LBJ**)
Operation Mongoose terminated
May 16: Tape of Hoffa loan to Estes
July: CM makes "cut the head off the dog" comment to Edward Becker
in reference to JFK
August: Estes estate bought
Break-in of Judith Campbell's apartment
End of Judith Campbell and JFK relationship
September: JEH tapes CM about contract on JFK
LHO works for FBI
ST tells Jose Aleman that JFK will be hit
Increased relations between Judith Campbell and SG
October 31: Supreme Court refuses to hear CM case
November 23: Decision on TFX (F111) aircraft
November 24: Secretary of Defense Robert McNamara announces TFX
decision

1963 January: Judith Campbell has abortion arranged by SG
Mob calls for elimination of JFK
January 27: LHO buys revolver
March: JF meets LHO
March 12: LHO buys rifle
March 21: Many questions regarding TFX plane to JFK
March 28: Estes conviction
April: SG and rogue elements of the CIA plan JFK assassination
April 10: Attempt to assassinate Gen. Edwin Walker
May 27: Mafia families furious with JFK
Supreme Court again refuses to hear CM case
June: Original planning of JFK assassination by Mafia

Time Line

June 5: JFK discusses November trip to Texas
June 18: Break between RFK and LBJ
July: Hoffa claims JFK must be eliminated
August: LHO, David Ferrie, Clay Shaw travel to Clinton, LA
August 9: LHO in jail
August 20: Questions about Secretary of the Navy Fred Korth regarding
    TFX plane
September 13: Dallas papers report that JFK will visit
September 17: Public admonished to be "congenial" hosts in Dallas
September 25: Silvio Odio meets "Leon Oswald"
Joseph Valachi testifies to Senate committee
September 26: LHO to Mexico City?
October 2: Meeting of Joint Chiefs of Staff on Vietnam
October 4: Stars and Stripes report of troops to be out of Vietnam
October 11: NSAM no. 263 issued
October 24: Hostile treatment of Adlai Stevenson in Dallas
November: South Vietnam's president Ngo Dinh Diem murdered
November 1: Korth resigns as secretary of the navy
Case of *U.S. vs. Carlos Marcello* begins
Plans for JFK to visit Tampa and Miami
November 8: LHO writes to "Mr. Hunt"?
November 9: Joseph Milteer outlines plans of how JFK will be killed
November 17: JF to Dallas
November 20: Rose Cheramie reports to authorities that JFK will be
    killed
November 21: *New York Times* reports troops to be out of Vietnam
Defense of CM case rests
JFK "wanted" posters appear in Dallas
Party in Dallas of JFK enemies
JFK departs for Texas
LHO asks friend for ride to take curtain rods
November 22: 2:00–3:00 a.m.: Secret Service detail at The Cellar nightclub
LHO carries "curtain rods" to work
CM acquitted
    11:50 a.m.: JFK departs from Love Field, Dallas
    12:30 p.m.: Secret Service notices clock on Texas School Book
        Depository (**TSBD**), JFK shot
    12:31 p.m.: Police check out LHO
    12:34 p.m.: Inspector J. Herbert Sawyer in TSBD

12:40 p.m.: LHO leaves the TSBD

1:00 p.m.: JFK pronounced dead at Parkland Memorial Hospital

1:00 p.m.: Police Capt. Will J. Fritz takes charge of investigation; LHO arrives at rooming house

1:02 p.m.: Cartridge cases found on sixth floor of the school book warehouse

1:04 p.m.: LHO leaves rooming house

1:15 p.m.: Dallas Police Officer J. D. Tippit killed

1:16 p.m.: Police notified of Tippit's death

1:22 p.m.: Rifle and shells found in TSBD

1:40 p.m.: Police called from Texas Theater in the Oak Cliff neighborhood

1:45 p.m.: Police enter theater and arrest LHO

2:38 p.m.: LBJ sworn in as president

3:00 p.m.: Police visit Ruth Paine and LHO's wife, Marina

5:58 p.m.: Air Force One arrives at Andrews Air Force Base with JFK's body

7:10 p.m.: Police charge LHO with Officer Tippit's murder

November 23: Revolver found near grassy knoll; New Orleans newspaper headlines acquittal of CM rather than assassination of JFK

1:30 a.m.: LHO charged with murder of JFK

November 24: 11:00 a.m.: Arrival of armored car at Dallas Police Department basement for transfer of LHO to county jail

11:17 a.m.: Jack Ruby enters Dallas Police Department basement

11:21 a.m.: LHO shot

11:27 a.m.: LHO arrives at Parkland Memorial Hospital

1:13 p.m.: LHO pronounced dead

November 25: Calls by LBJ for service on Warren Commission

November 26: NSAM no. 273: troops to remain in Vietnam

November 29: Warren Commission constituted to investigate JFK assassination

December 16: Lee Rankin as general counsel for Assassination Committee

December 17: FBI document mentions LHO with a symbol

1964   August: RFK resigns as U.S. Attorney General

September 24: Report of Warren Commission released

1965   April 22: RFK releases JFK brain to Evelyn Lincoln in National Archives

May: SG refuses to talk, sent to jail in Cook County, Illinois

Time Line

1966 CIA director denies the agency ever plotted to assassinate Castro
May: SG released from jail
October 31: Burke Marshall finds no JFK brain

1967 January 3: Jack Ruby dies of cancer
February 22: David Ferrie dies, his CIA paymaster killed

1968 August: Ferrie's roommate reveals his involvement with LHO

1970 October 25: Gen. Rene Schneider murdered in Chile

1973 December 20: R Cain murdered

1974 July: Antoinette Giancana tells SG she plans to file for divorce
SG leaves Mexican estate
December: *New York Times* reports that CIA violated charter

1975 April 7: Nelson Rockefeller chairs hearing on CIA assassinations
May 30: Unnamed CIA chief testifies to Frank Church's Senate
    Committee
June 6: SG meets with Tony Acardo and Joseph Aiuppa to confirm he is
    in good standing
June 9: Two CIA chiefs discuss need for Mafia help before Church
    Committee
June 19: *Chicago Tribune* and *New York Times* report CIA scheme to
    poison Castro
Staff of Church Committee in Chicago to escort SG to Washington for
    his appearance before the committee
    9:00 p.m.: Neighbors see two "law enforcement officers" outside SG's
        home
    9:30–9:45 p.m.: Daughter Francine and Butch Blasi leave SG's home
    10:15 p.m.: Blasi returns with daughter Connie Sue
    11:00 p.m.: SG prepares snack
    11:15 p.m.: SG sees three surveillance cars leave
    11:30 p.m.: SG murdered
    11:52 p.m.: Caretaker discovers SG's body
    11:53 p.m.: Call from the Giancana house to Oak Park Police
June 20: 1:40 a.m.: SG taken to Oak Park Hospital ER
    1:45 a.m.: SG declared dead
Chicago Tribune reports SG's murder
Allegations made that SG's murder was sanctioned by CIA
June 21: *Chicago Tribune* reports SG's house under surveillance the night
    he was killed

June 24: Johnny Rosselli testifies before Church Committee
Planned appearance of SG at Church Committee
July: Admission by JFK adviser McGeorge Bundy in Church Committee
   regarding assassinations
July 22: Inquest into SG murder
July 23: Gen. George Smathers reports JFK's reaction to his Cuba
   discussion
July 29: Robert Maheu testifies before Church Committee
July 30: Jimmy Hoffa disappears
August: Castro gives senator evidence of twenty-four attempts on his life
November: Church Committee releases findings

1976   July 6: NSAM no. 263 declassified
   July 27: Rosselli warned to get out of Miami
   July 28: Rosselli killed
   August 7: Rosselli's body found
   September: U.S. House committee investigates JFK's and Martin Luther
      King Jr.'s assassinations

1977   Chuckie Nicoletti killed; George DeMohrenschildt commits "suicide"

1978   March: One of Hoffa's killers killed

1979   U.S. House of Representatives Assassination Committee report

1987   John C. Rademacher finds casing on grassy knoll overlooking Dealey
   Plaza in Dallas
   May 13: ST dying, confesses involvement in JFK assassination
   May 17: ST dies

1988   TV interview with Judith Campbell

1992   January 15: Oliver Stone speaks to National Press Club

1993   May 3: JF reveals teeth marks on casings
   October 4: Dentist reveals human teeth marks on shell

1994   March 22: Taped interview of JF

1997   June 24: Letter from Antoinette Giancana to JF
   July 1: Letter from JF to Antoinette Giancana

Index

Index

Index

McNamara, Robert S., 155–57, 160
McNeil, Robert, 182
McWillie, Louis, 110, 113, 171
military-industrial complex, 55,
    59–60, 88, 158, 161, 163, 217
Milteer, Joseph, 21, 89, 185, 187
Minacore, Calogaros, 141
Minacore, Luigia, 139
Minh, Duong Van, 118
Mirro, James "Cowboy," 77–78, 80,
    93, 211
Mollenhoff, Clark R., 117
Mondale, Walter, 124
Monroe, Marilyn, 105, 169
Mooney, Luke, 28, 97, 99
Morris, W. R., 187
Murchison, Clint, Sr., 21, 173, 178
Murret, Charles "Dutz," 113, 145,
    177, 179, 187

National Security Action Memos
    No. 55, 158, 163
    No. 56, 159
    No. 57, 159
    No. 263, 88, 160–63
New Orleans, LA, 60, 76, 86, 88–89,
    91, 104, 109, 112–13, 139–43,
    145–46, 170, 173–74, 177, 179, 186,
    203, 212
Nicoletti, Chuckie, 80, 90–91, 112,
    173, 189–92, 195–97, 200, 202, 204,
    212
Nitti, Frank, 184
Nixon, Richard M., 22, 102–4, 114,
    118, 132, 134, 155
North, Mark, 165–66

O'Day, J., 28, 183
Odio, Silvia, 89, 179, 187

O'Donnell, Kenneth, 19, 168, 186–87
Ogilvie, Richard, 114
Oliver, Beverly, 184
Olivier, Alfred G., 34
Ommaya, A. K., 193
Oswald, Lee Harvey, 25–29, 31, 35–36,
    38–40, 48–51, 53–55, 59–61, 75, 80,
    88–89, 112–13, 143, 145–46, 177–
    88, 190, 192–95, 197, 199, 202–3,
    213, 217
Oswald, Leon (alias for Lee Harvey
    Oswald), 59, 89, 179, 187

Paine, Ruth, 28
Parkland, Memorial Hospital (Dallas,
    TX), 24, 28–29, 34, 36–37, 44, 55
Parrott, Thomas, 152
Partin, Edward, 170
Patrick, Lenny, 174
Patterson, John, 118
Pearson, Drew, 77
Perry, Malcolm O., 34
Phillips, David Atlee, 190, 192, 195,
    202, 204, 213
Pitzer, William B., 185
Plumlee, William Robert "Posh," 203
Pool, Joe, 20
Poretto, Joe, 145
Posner, Gerald, 61
Postal, Julia, 27
Prouty, Fletcher, 54–55, 59–60,
    149–50, 155, 157, 161–63, 202
Provenzano, Anthony "Tough Tony,"
    136

Quigley, John Lester, 179

Raab, Selwyn, 129
Rademacher, John C., 205

Index

Index

About the Authors

ANTOINETTE GIANCANA is the daughter of Mafia chief Sam Giancana, who controlled Chicago in the late 1950s and early 1960s. He was likely the major player at that time in organized crime in the United States and later expanded his empire to Europe and the Middle East. As his daughter, Antoinette knew her father well, knew his colleagues and friends, like Frank Sinatra, and was married to Bob McDonnell, a lawyer for the Chicago mob and close associate of Sam Giancana. She has the best qualifications of anyone alive today to relate what her father said and what he did. Furthermore, she has written a book, *Mafia Princess,* that was on the bestseller list for twelve weeks, culminating in a popular movie with the same name, featuring Tony Curtis as Sam and Susan Lucci as Antoinette. Antoinette has appeared in interviews scores of times, not only in the United States, especially on national networks, but also in England and recently in France. Her comments have never been challenged, because she has related truthfully what she saw and heard. Recently, Tina Sinatra wrote a book about her father, *My Father's Daughter,* and claimed that her father introduced Sam Giancana to Joseph Patrick Kennedy, who made an appeal for Giancana's help to elect John F. Kennedy to the White House. Antoinette's husband was, in fact, the one who brought Sam Giancana to Judge Tuohy's office in Chicago and made the introduction.

JOHN R. HUGHES, DM Oxon, MD, PhD, has written 7 books and 503 scientific medical articles about the brain and its function. He is the director of clinical neurophysiology, director of the epilepsy center, and professor of neurology at the University of Illinois Medical Center in Chicago. As a professor of neurology, he brings his expertise in explaining why Kennedy's body could not have been slammed to his left because of a reflex from a bullet into the right hemisphere of his brain, shot from behind, such as from the book depository. In his professional life he has lectured to the state's attorneys of Illinois on medical-legal matters and also to large groups of practicing attorneys in the medical-legal community, served as an editor on a journal dealing with these matters. He has been called upon by the state's attorney's office to testify in many murder trials in Cook County, Illinois. The two major high-profile trials include that of Richard Speck, who killed eight nurses one night in Chicago. Brain-wave tests were run on Speck, and Dr. Hughes gave testimony in the trial that helped to convict Speck to a life sentence. The second high-profile case was that of John Wayne Gacy, who killed at least thirty-five young men in the Chicago area. Dr. Hughes was asked to plan, arrange, and coordinate all of the medical data in this case, including brain-wave tests, which he analyzed. His findings helped to convict Gacy for many of his murders. Finally, Dr. Hughes has spent more than ten years reading at least forty books on the Kennedy assassination and has given considerable thought to the events in Dallas and the events that led to the assassinations of John F. Kennedy and Sam Giancana. He has an MD from Northwestern University and a PhD from Harvard University. In 1976 Oxford University honored Dr. Hughes with the rarely awarded degree Doctor of Medicine.

THOMAS H. JOBE, MD, is professor of psychiatry and associate director of neuropsychiatry at the University of Illinois Medical Center in Chicago. He did graduate work in the history of science and medicine at the University of Chicago after becoming a psychiatrist, and this expertise in history accounted for the success of his book (with Professor Hyman L. Muslim) *Lyndon Baines Johnson: The Tragic Self: A PsychoHistorical Portrayal*. Dr. Jobe's book deals with LBJ's early life as a key to explain Johnson's personal characteristics. This book is an excellent example of a popular book form called psychohistory. Dr. Jobe's expertise in human behavior and psychiatry is important in this book, since there is a concerted attempt to make all motivations consistent with the personalities of the major players. Thus the actions and motivations behind these actions have made good psychiatric sense to Dr. Jobe.